Grow Your Own

PENICILLIN

Words Prescribed for a Happy and Healthy Spirit

STORIES, DEVOTIONS, AND POEMS

Ellenor Shepherd

WESTBOW
PRESS
A DIVISION OF THOMAS NELSON

WestBow Press books may be ordered through booksellers or by contacting:

WestBow Press
A Division of Thomas Nelson
1663 Liberty Drive
Bloomington, IN 47403
www.westbowpress.com
1-(866) 928-1240

ISBN: 978-1-4497-7749-4 (e)
ISBN: 978-1-4497-7750-0 (sc)
ISBN: 978-1-4497-6969-7 (hc)

Library of Congress Control Number: 2012922527

Printed in the United States of America

WestBow Press rev. date: 12/06/2012

To my grandchildren,

**Harrison Flynn; Grace, Amelie, and
Peter Shepherd; and Clay Lanford.**

ACKNOWLEDGMENTS

To Lisa Moore, my "household engineer," who weekly teases me about growing mold in my refrigerator, thus triggering the idea for the title of this book ... I am forever grateful.

And to my family and several friends who provided a cache of material for these words, I give a special thanks for their faithfulness, their zest for living, and their willingness to tell all.

To my daughter-in-law, Molly Shepherd, my son, Dr. Clif Flynn, my church friend, Dr. Andy Mitchum, and my dear friend, Barbara Heilig, who edited this book. My gratitude is boundless.

To my other sons, John Shepherd and Dr. Wes Shepherd, who have faithfully supported and encouraged me to pursue my dreams. I treasure your confidence in me.

And, as always, to Lisa Whisenant, who, with her technical and communication skills, and her patience, rescues and saves my life as she fine-tunes my efforts. A lifetime of thanks.

CONTENTS

PREFACE

Each week Lisa, my delightful "household engineer," greets me by opening the refrigerator door and saying, "Well, what are you growing penicillin for this week?"

This has become a ritual, especially since I am notorious for never throwing anything away, even though I'm aware of the ugly mold attacking my cache of food.

In defense, I quickly say, "Penicillin is a good mold and has saved many lives. As a matter of fact, it was called the miracle drug at one time."

Of course, we should take it only if prescribed by our doctor. And it's of utmost importance to complete the dosage; otherwise, new bacteria will be allowed to develop.

Hey, isn't this what happens in our lives? Sometimes the bad mold takes over; sometimes we don't do what God says. God wants us to grow our own penicillin, with His help, of course. He wants us to learn to find our own good prescriptions, those that give us encouragement, courage, hope, joy, compassion, wisdom, strength, gratitude, and all the things that make our lives healthy and well.

Daily doses of penicillin, reminders of God's amazing love and power, definitely "gift" us with a healthy spirit.

PS: And if you should be allergic to penicillin, just find another good mold like I did!

INTRODUCTION

The stories, poems, and devotions in this book were written over a period of years as a result of many diverse experiences in my life. Some were joyful; some were sad. There were times of hurt, times of surprise, times of questioning, and times that dealt with many of the things life throws your way.

I have learned that in order to have a healthy spirit, we must listen to the doctor, God, and to grow our own penicillin, we must allow what we do to be Christ centered.

You are invited to step into each story, savor each word, and then let it speak to you and whatever you might be experiencing in your life at that time.

Give in to your feelings as you read. Find relief in tears of release. Enjoy the stress-cleaning laughter that produces healing endorphins. Rest in the contemplative moments which can lift you up, offering encouragement and hope, or simply a place to be.

These words are intended to touch your heart, open your mind, strengthen your faith, and encourage you to hold God's hand in everything you do.

I strongly urge you to write or discover, with God's directions, your own devotions, stories, and poems. In other words, *Grow Your Own Penicillin.*

SECTION 1
THOUGHTS FOR DEVOTIONS, MEDITATIONS, OR JUST THINKING

Rx: for Restored Energy

My Bathtub Retreat

A haven ... a sanctuary ... a rest stop ... an oasis ... a place of solitude ... a place to shed tears ... an energizer ... a place to wash away tears.

When my children were small, the luxury of privacy was found only in my bathroom. Once the door closed, they knew that the bath was off limits and dared not disturb Mom.

It continues to be my retreat, even though my three sons have grown up and no longer live at home and my husband and I have been divorced for several years; obvious quiet now pervades this entire space I call home.

Yet I still retreat to my bathtub, perhaps out of habit, and I like to think of it as one of those "holy ordinary" places that gives meaning to my life. Whenever I crawl into my tub, a pen and pad are inevitably placed on a towel on the side of the tub just in case I am inspired with a special thought, idea, or revelation. This has happened more times than I can remember.

In this ordinary white, porcelain vessel, I have written a Christmas play, poetry, and parts of a book; read many novels; prayed; given freedom to my thoughts; and just relaxed.

What is so special about this old, white tub, which at times evokes such an outpouring of creativity that even I am surprised? At other times, it compels me to lower myself into the warm water and simply savor its restorative power.

I will find peace in my bathtub, a place where I am naked before God with all my imperfections, both physical and spiritual, without even a fig leaf. I am free to be me and free simply to be and feel His presence.

3

Rx: for Elimination

Weeding as Prayer Song

Pulling ... digging ... clipping. Sweating ... panting ... groaning. This is my aria, my solo, my offering, my peaceful straining to coexist with this amazing symphonic interlude in my out-of-doors life.

This struggle to run with the weeds is never ending. Forever invading ... forever threatening ... forever marring the beauty.

And yet how else could I harmonize so completely with the dove that calls and the chipmunks, rabbit, and squirrels frolicking and eating their day through my yard?

Both wildlife and I together, attuned with the wind gently blowing through the trees, delicately teasing the several wind chimes that seem to chant words of encouragement.

And finally a small patch of garden, clean and free of these offensive intruders.

Free now to reach out and grow, free now to radiate its beauty, free to be shared with others.

I have been given a gift, a sense of oneness with my Creator, and He didn't even seem to mind that I was covered with dirt!

Dear God,

Help us to remember that we will always have weeds in our lives to choke out the good, to distract, to cause us to stray. Give us the wisdom to recognize these invaders and the strength to remove them at the proper time from our garden of life.

We love You, Lord. Amen.

Rx: for Emotional Stability

My "Crumby" Day

My basket runneth over!
　　I can barely lift it.
Heavy with the weight of today's crumbs
Unexpectedly confronting me,
　　Demanding my attention,
Revealing itself to me,
Touching my innermost being,
Daring me to recognize the preciousness of the gift.
　　The touch, the word, the everyday, seemingly
　　unnecessary
And tiring trivialities, and yes, the unkindness—even the
hurt.
　　Each waiting to be embraced, to be accepted as a
　　blessing,
To be received as nourishment, to feel the presence.
　　Yes, my basket runneth over and I thank God for
　　My "crumby" day.

*At the end of each day, take the time to gather the crumbs
and count your many unique and unexpected blessings. (How
about a gratitude journal?)*

Rx: for Loss of Voice

I Didn't Say, "Good Morning, Lord"

I didn't say, "Good morning, Lord." Why? It dawned on me while I was taking my warm bath this morning that so many times I haven't said, "Good morning." I would never do that to my family. When I get up, I always speak to my children and husband and anyone else who is in the house. I *always* say, "Good morning."

Why did I not say, "Good morning," to You? I can't imagine how I could be so remiss, Lord. And when I realized what I had done all these years, it made me so sad, and I had such regrets, such remorse, that I actually shed tears when I thought about it.

I should have known that I needed You to start my days, but I was too busy focusing on other things. Guess I was focusing mainly on me and the things that were not very productive, at least not in the sense that You perceive production.

I don't know, Lord; there's a big loss here. As I said, I can't go back and make up for lost time, but I just know that I never want to be in that position again. And I hope You'll nudge me on the days I'm slow to get started. I hope You will remind me, Father, to look to You for guidance for my day, just as I try to guide my own children.

I am still shocked and in a state of disbelief that I didn't say, "Good morning," to You ... my own Father. How that must have hurt and disappointed You. And You never complain, Lord. You just keep on loving me and forgiving me, and I keep on taking.

It has taken a long time to wake me up, hasn't it, Lord? Oh, You know that I have always loved You and, of course, turned to You in times of need. (Don't most of us?) And, yes, I often prayed but not on a regular basis. I was easily sidetracked, and many times I actually gave You the answer.

But Lord, from now on, please know that as long as You are in my home and in my heart, I'll always say, "Good morning, Lord!"

Rx: for Encouraging

Have I Known a Barnabas?
Have I Been a Barnabas?

Everyone—man, woman, mother, father, son, daughter, sister, brother, grandson, granddaughter, relative, friend, casual acquaintance, stranger, leader, the rich, the poor, the weak, the strong, the learned, the illiterate—needs a Barnabas.

And ... everyone needs to be a Barnabas!

In Acts 11:22–24, we read,

> When he arrived and saw the evidence of the Grace of God, he was glad and encouraged them all to remain true to the Lord with all their hearts. He was a good man, full of the Holy Spirit and faith, and a great number of people were brought to the Lord.

Surely to be an encourager is one of the most needed and effective of our spiritual gifts. It requires no special training, no advanced studies, and no great leadership skills. It has no age, sex, or race limitations, and we do not need permission to use it. This means if we refuse to be an encourager, we would definitely carry a lame excuse.

The timid need encouraging. The person with little or no confidence responds to an encourager. The person who is unsure of her direction benefits from a simple word of encouragement. The patient who is fighting a hard battle finds strength from an encourager. A child learning to read progresses more rapidly with words of encouragement. Everyone needs an encourager! Everyone needs a Barnabas!

I am convinced that the greatest temptation in our everyday lives is to criticize or belittle our families, our friends, our coworkers, and anyone else who crosses our path, as well as those we know through work, the news media, and yes, even hearsay.

Sometimes just one little word or phrase can destroy someone for a lifetime. To say, "You're bad" to a child may determine his or her future actions. "If you can't stay within the lines, you might as well not color" might squelch a budding artist. "Can't you ever do anything right" regarding a spilled glass of milk or an error in judgment can reduce a child or adult to a nonentity.

To constantly criticize your spouse plants a wedge that circumvents a good relationship. To find fault with an employee by belittling his efforts destroys his self-confidence and kills the desire to even try. To put down a leader and others in control often undermines their effectiveness. To demean a person who finds himself alone in his ideas or lifestyle often causes him to be more withdrawn and even consider and/or commit suicide.

To criticize is an unwelcomed discouragement which can produce destructive and long-lasting consequences.

Take time now to stop and recall an incident in the past, no matter how insignificant it may seem, when someone unexpectedly surprised you by a word of encouragement—even if it was nothing but "Good job" or "You always do your best," or even if that person was not entirely pleased: "You're improving" or "I think you're good at what you do."

Have You Known a Barnabas?

What was your reaction to the words you remember? My guess is that you wanted to try harder, to do better, to please more, and to feel good about yourself. Your self-esteem was given a boost, and hopefully you were motivated to encourage someone else.

Isn't it amazing how "badness begets badness" and "goodness begets goodness"?

Have You Known a Barnabas?

There are times when it is necessary or important to point out someone's shortcomings, but that most likely will not be well received unless you have first built a relationship of trust. Then comes the realization that your words are never spoken out of unkindness but instead because you care.

This person we know as "encourager" usually does her encouraging in private, does not flaunt her role, if in fact she is even aware of this subtle yet powerful influence. She is often overlooked when committees are formed, positions are being filled, and important decisions must be made. Yet she probably would be the catalyst that jump-starts with the "trusted words of encouragement," a mood, a seemingly impossible task, a reluctance to cooperate, or most any difficult situation.

Have You Known a Barnabas?

This encourager, this "son of encouragement," has been blessed with this precious gift, and because of his willingness to take a risk, our lives have often undoubtedly been transformed.

And most of the time we are even unaware of this quietly effective servant: "the encourager."

Have You Known a Barnabas?

Can we too be a Barnabas and be an encourager to others?

Have I been a Barnabas?

Rx: for Painful Feet

Forgive My Trampling

How often I must have trampled on You, oh Lord. I didn't even have the courtesy to walk around You. Instead, I crushed You under my footsteps with no thought of the pain and suffering I inflicted. I was so focused on my own needs that I was unaware of what I had done. Why didn't I at least say, "Excuse me, Lord, but I don't have time for You right now. I have more important things that need my attention" or, "Just hang around, Lord. I may have some free time later on today"? Or I could have said, "I really don't want to hear what You are saying to me, Lord. I don't want to think about that. It doesn't make me feel good about myself."

And every day, many times a day, I trampled and trampled on You, Lord, and You didn't stop me. You actually allowed me to behave in this shameful manner and You never corrected me, lectured me, or pointed Your finger at me. Maybe You did, and I was blind and deaf (self-centered, I believe it's called). I only trampled on and on, causing You more suffering and pain.

No wonder that my feet hurt, with pain so unbearable at times that I can barely walk. The slightest pressure often brings me to tears, and I wonder why this is happening to me. I think I understand now, Lord. It is Your pain that I feel in my feet; it is the hurt that You are suffering; it is the agony of my own sinful weight as I trample on You.

The horror is that I am not the only one trampling on You; however, this "safety in numbers" or "misery loves company" thing offers me no consolation whatsoever. It only magnifies far beyond my comprehension, this crushing weight of humanity—Your own creation—that tramples on You without ceasing. No wonder You felt the need to send Your Son to save us from our sin-filled ways. And, sadly, we trample on Him.

Dear God,

Help us learn that we need to put You first, to find time during the day to just sit and listen, to take time to study Your word, to put our own selfish wants aside, to ask what You would have us do.

And Lord, please forgive me for constantly trampling on You and causing You unimaginable pain.

In Jesus' name, I love You, Lord.

Amen.

Rx: for Blurred Vision

I Didn't Know You, Lord

*If a stranger approached you and said he was
the Messiah, would you believe him?*

I Didn't Know You, Lord.

I had heard that You were coming, Lord, that You might already be here, but why haven't I seen You?

I've tried to be a good person. I attend church regularly, teach Sunday school, and volunteer in many other ways. I'm a good neighbor; I haven't killed anyone, maybe gossiped a little—well, more than a little. I've been good to my mother and daddy, and on occasion, I have wanted what my friends have; perhaps a few choice words have escaped my lips. I try to tell the truth, Lord, but sometimes I might stretch it a bit so that I will look good in Your eyes. I thought surely You would want to introduce Yourself to me. I really don't have time to go out searching for You.

Yesterday I was rushing out of the grocery store and some church people who were soliciting food for the poor asked me for a donation, but I was in too much of a hurry to go back, buy more groceries, and get in line again.

I Didn't Know You, Lord.

I noticed a man standing alone, off to one side in the Fellowship Hall at church. He kept shifting from one foot to another; his hair was pulled back in a ponytail; his clothes needed pressing, for sure. I really did not want to get involved by speaking to him for fear that it might have led to directing him somewhere or introducing him to someone. Besides, my friends were waiting by the coffee table and I was eager to join them.

I Didn't Know You, Lord.

Three young neighborhood children rang my doorbell right in the middle of my struggling efforts to make a cake. I had just looked up as they trampled through my flowerbed. When I answered the door, they excitedly asked if I would like to buy some flowers (probably from my own garden). I said, "No, I already have flowers, and please do not bother me again." I couldn't help but notice how crestfallen and disappointed they looked, even though they politely thanked me.

I Didn't Know You, Lord.

I had just sat down to read my morning paper when the phone rang and I answered. When I heard the voice on the other end, I thought, *Oh no, not today, please.* It was my ninety-year-old friend who must have the strength of a gorilla in her arms to hold the phone to her ear 'til doomsday. Here come the stories. I can lip-sync with her, I have heard them so many times. And besides, it keeps me from falling asleep. Once in a while, I will penetrate the droning with one of those little white lies ... "Someone is at my door," I say, and it doesn't even slow her down. Later, I might say, "I really need to go to the bathroom." Again, no let up. Finally, I might say, "I have an appointment in fifteen minutes and must get dressed. Talk to you later. Bye."

I Didn't Know You, Lord.

One of my sons, grungy from playing in his special dirt pile, runs into the house and gives me a great big bear hug. "Don't touch me!" I scream as I jump away. "Can't you see I'm dressed to go to my bridge club? Why didn't you think before you jumped all over me, as dirty as you are?" He put his head down and slinked away.

I Didn't Know You, Lord.
How many times have I missed You?

Were You actually smiling at me in the grocery store when I was asked for food and I looked the other way?

Were You the stranger standing to the side in the Fellowship Hall at church, just longing for a friendly hello, an extended hand?

Were You the phone call testing my patience with the exhausting, long conversation, trying to get my attention?

Were You the young children who rang my doorbell, so excited about selling me flowers, and I chastised You for disturbing me?

Could You have possibly been my own son with dirty hands who tried to wrap his arms around me, and I pushed You away?

I Didn't Know You, Lord.

I ignored the poor, excluded the stranger, dampened the spirits of young children, resented the call of the lonely, older friend, and rejected my own son.

And I thought I was worthy of a visit from You, Lord.

No, I am most definitely not worthy, but it certainly is more than apparent how very much I need You. How I need Your forgiveness. How I long to know how it feels to have Your loving arms wrapped around me. How I want to hear Your stories, Lord. How I want to make you feel welcomed in my home.

But most of all, Lord, I want to recognize you in others. I want to be able to say,

I Know You, Lord.

Most patient Lord,

Peel back the curtains from my eyes so that I might know You in whatever shape or form You appear. Constantly remind me that all I need to do is look for You in others. Amen.

Rx: for Hearing Problems

The Silence

As I sit quietly in my den, I hear the flames in my fireplace rushing upward in their hushed rhythm. I hear the creaking bones of a fifty-one-year-old house. Sometimes, I will hear the constant chirping of a lone cricket that sneaked uninvited into my solitude.

If I am on my porch, I am attuned to the wind rushing through the pines, the squirrels scampering from tree to tree, the birds singing and scratching the dirt for survival, the wonderful sounds of children next door, and the cars racing by. None of these are distracting as they lurk in the background and go unnoticed until they are welcomed into my world of silence.

At night, the silence takes on different sounds. Nature is stilled. The night clouds move silently, breathing lightly as they go by. A snapping twig may startle me. I become aware of my watch ticking, if I rest my head on my arm, the rumble of my tummy, and my own breathing as I listen with anticipation.

But so often when I enter the silence, voices bombard me with thoughts and memories I cannot seem to stifle.

And then sometimes, when I am still and focus and "just be," a quiet voice whispers to me, capturing my attention, making me hunger for so much more. And I believe in that moment I shall always welcome this Presence with my heart, an open mind, and open arms. But being the human that I am, I disappoint myself by allowing many other things to come between me, my silence and the presence, and I can't help but wonder that God once again also feels disappointed.

It's the silence between the notes that makes the music.

Ancient Zen Proverb

SECTION 2
LIFE'S LITTLE LESSONS

Rx: for Coping

Don't Rock the Boat

When I returned from church last Sunday morning, the light was blinking on my answering machine. I pushed the play button and was greeted by the booming, rich voice of my son, John, who lives in Asheville.

"Good morning, Mom. I just passed by a church with these words on their marquee: 'Calm seas do not make a skillful sailor.' Hope you have a wonderful day. I love you."

Wow! Eight words packed with a powerful and thought-provoking message.
Right. How can we possibly learn without challenges along life's way?
Thank you, Lord, for rough seas.
(Why don't you expand on this thought!)

"One man's courage makes a majority."

Andrew Jackson

Rx: for Ophidiophobia (Fear of Snakes)

Ungrounded Fears

Several years ago, my five-year-old grandson was visiting and I, trying to be a good grandmother, took him out to the Country Park Petting Zoo. Harrison was fascinated with all the animals and the fact that he was allowed to touch them.

The adventure was going quite smoothly until the teacher/guide reached into a cage and removed a long, black snake. It was all I could do not to run away since I have always had a paralyzing fear of this creature. Harrison, on the other hand, could hardly wait until it was his turn to gently rub the snake. He was thrilled!

Trying to cover my fear and discomfort, I made the unretractable mistake of saying, "I promised myself that before I die, I am going to touch a snake."

And the handler looked me straight in the eye and replied, "What better time than now?" I was horrified at the thought, but my grandson was waiting eagerly for me to have the same enjoyable experience that he had. With trembling hands, knees, and every other part of me, I timidly reached out and touched that frightening reptile. To my surprise, I liked the feel. It was not slimy as I had long imagined; it felt almost like velvet. I was actually thrilled that at age sixty-seven I could finally boast that I had petted a snake! Miracles never cease!

The moral: Don't judge a book by its cover. Or don't judge someone by a first impression. Or reach out to someone who is different or has a different color or background. Or ... (Try writing your own lesson learned.)

A Small, Quiet Voice

While visiting my Richmond family, my daughter-in-law, Molly, and I succumbed to our usual desire to go shopping. Of course my two granddaughters, Grace and Amelie, were included in this outing and were busily holding court on their backseat thrones in the SUV.

Unfortunately, my restless leg syndrome, which constantly plagues me, kicked in at that time and I must have pitifully groaned that fact to Molly. Suddenly, during a brief lull in the conversation, a small voice from the backseat quietly spoke these words: "Grammie, maybe you should talk to God about that."

Out of the mouths of babes ...

In nine words, four-year-old Grace brought me to my knees and touched my very soul with her childlike faith. I shall never forget that small, quiet voice and its powerful message.

I believe that children are our most overlooked disciples.

Rx: for Anxiety

Riding the Rails

It had been years since I had traveled by train, so a slight feeling of apprehension lurked in the background as I boarded the Amtrak in Richmond, Virginia.

My daughter-in-law had packed a goody bag for my enjoyment since the trip was scheduled to be five hours long. I quickly settled down in the spacious seat and began reading my book. Occasionally, I would glance out the window at the passing countryside.

About forty-five minutes into the trip, I felt the train slowing down and was surprised to see that we were in the middle of nowhere. The conductor's voice boomed over the loudspeaker, informing us that we were stopping to pick up a passenger. This accomplished, we were on our way, or so I thought. But in approximately thirty minutes, this same booming voice announced, apologetically, that we needed to pull onto a side track to allow an oncoming train to pass. Needless to say, I was grateful for small favors; however, after learning that much of the way we had only one set of tracks, my apprehension intensified.

The train passed by (very close, I might add), and we took off again. Just as we rolled into the city of Rocky Mount, North Carolina, this now familiar booming voice came over the speaker again. "Ladies and gentlemen, I'm afraid we might have an extended delay. The train directly in front of us has broken down, and unfortunately, it is where there is only one track. As soon as they get the new part and can pull up, we will be able to go around them on the second track." After a two-hour delay, we proceeded to our destination, Greensboro, North Carolina, finally arriving at 9 p.m.

In the meantime, a visibly irritated lady passenger called her brother to come and rescue her, so she aborted the trip. Another lady, who was visiting from Australia, was understandably distressed to learn that she would miss the James Galway concert. The young boy and girl traveling with their parents were convinced that they were imprisoned.

At last, we arrived at our intended destination, intact though a bit weary.

My dear and patient friends, who were to pick me up and with whom I had been in cell phone contact, filled their time by eating, riding around (burning precious gas), and finally collapsing in the beautifully restored train station.

In retrospect, I thought, *What a play on our lives.* How many times are we sidetracked when we are trying to accomplish something or when we are trying to do the right thing? How often do we have to stop to pick up a passenger or find that our well-made plans are interrupted? And how often in our life's journey have big obstacles suddenly appeared in our path, causing us to look for a way to bypass or deal with them? It may be pain, disappointment, hurt, an unexpected job loss, move, divorce, or ...

But like the train engineer, we have to learn to deal with these unplanned, irritating, and sometimes life-changing circumstances that we had not anticipated.

We can be accepting and make life better, or we can be resentful, blame God, and be bitter.

I have found that from every bad experience I have encountered, I have learned an invaluable lesson, and it has made me a stronger and a more compassionate and understanding person.

Now I thank God each time I must face an unexpected and unwanted blow, knowing that if I trust Him, He will give me the strength to cope and good things will grow out of it.

My Amtrak train ride helped me to focus on two things: God is in control and God is with me in any and every situation.

I can hardly wait for my next opportunity to "ride the rails."

"Trust in the Lord with all your heart, and lean not unto your own understanding. In all your ways acknowledge Him, and He will direct your path."

Proverbs 3:5–6

Rx: for Bipolar Disorder

Living in Two Spaces

I live in another dimension, but my winter home is in reality. Living in two spaces is like having a dual personality. Which is the real me? Maybe that is the problem—I'm not sure who I am. Confusion settles in as I move back and forth between the two. Often the persons are as different as day and night, while at other times they collide and almost merge into one entity.

Do you dream of another life: living in a different place, in a different time, as a different person, with a different job, with different friends, or different interests? Perhaps a place where you are not judged, where you can do whatever your heart desires, where time is of no concern, where you can try new things without fear of failure, where you can enjoy an unquestioned schedule, where you are not accountable to anyone.

At first thought, I was positive that this would be a kind of utopia, a world which screamed joy and happiness. But as I examine each aspect of this new environment, this new planet (so to speak), my assuredness begins to falter, to question, to dissect the validity of such a place.

I certainly thought that I knew this place, this "another dimension," and all it entails, but suddenly, strange and puzzling concerns flash across my mind, leaving me in a jumbled and confused state.

I am like all humans, I imagine: desiring more than my share, wanting to have my way, living a riotous life with no consideration of my family or others, keeping material possessions for myself, abusing my body by filling it with unhealthy libations and foods, and, oh yes, ignoring the need for exercise. As for my spiritual side, I consider that the outdoors takes care of that dimension and places no demands on me and my other activities. What more could I possibly want?

And yet there is a void, an emptiness that keeps seeping into my world that I cannot quite fill, delete, understand, or identify. It continues to tug at my innermost being, evoking emotions that defy the other me. It pulls me back into reality, questioning my selfish and self-centered modes of behavior. It challenges me with the power of its honesty, sincerity, compassion, and love.

And I feel that transformation, with little regret, gently guiding me back to my winter home in reality, where I am blessed with such abundance that I can barely climb the steps under the weight into my refuge, my haven.

Once more I feel the Presence and am reminded that I am safe, happy, unconditionally loved, and in a space which welcomes me home, no matter where I might be.

"Trust (lean on, rely on, and be confident) in the Lord and do good; so shall you dwell in the land and feed surely on His faithfulness, and truly you shall be fed."

Psalm 37:3

Rx: for Acceptance

Comfort from My Hard Chair

Time loses all meaning as the day stretches into night in the hospital waiting room. I am nested in the hard chair, the typical chair with a short back and no padding in its seat, that I have claimed as mine.

I have surrounded myself with little things that could be squeezed into my tote bag, things that might, for a brief time, distract my anxious mind: knitting needles and yarn for a shawl; a crossword puzzle, barely touched (the words elude me); a book that once demanded my full attention; snacks; and a few other odds and ends.

After a while, legs begin to swell from dangling for hours. I can feel my shoes daring my feet to breathe.

People all around me are talking—some laughing, some crying, others staring with that knowing look until they too become almost invisible and mute to my world—and the only thing I am barely aware of is my hard chair.

Is there a special posture to assume while waiting for death to come to a loved one? Am I expected to use only certain words and no longer smile, or instead must I cry now and then to show that I care, to avoid being labeled as tough or unfeeling?

Dare I leave to pick up food that will be, at best, only nibbled? I don't know. I've never been instructed in "waiting for the dying to die." I've never been given ten easy steps. *I never was told that it takes a lifetime to wait for something you wish would never happen at all.*

And each time I am allowed that short visit to stand by the bedside, I wonder if my presence, even in silence, is acknowledged or if the machines obliterate my soft steps and quiet voice.

I reach out and touch an unresponsive hand, hoping at least for an eyelid to flutter—a sign, any sign, that says, "I'm glad you're here."

And then, back to that hard chair, my chair that has become a vital part of my existence.

Loved ones—family and friends—come and go, murmuring words of kindness, offering prayers, bringing food, magazines—gestures to show they care, gestures that don't go unnoticed, but that often touch a raw nerve ending that almost destroys my composure. I fight to keep the tears from flooding the halls.

They leave and I settle into my hard chair, my haven, until that next fifteen-minute visit comes, almost mocking me with its torturing slow arrival.

And I sit in my hard chair once again, hoping I will not be summoned to leave my chair for those dreaded words in that inevitable hour.

I find comfort from my hard chair ... another "holy ordinary" that gifts me in my deepest need.

In claiming something like an ordinary hard chair and allowing it to become our space away from home, we eventually find comfort in our acceptance.

Amen.

Rx: for Confusion

Worry versus Concern
Is there a difference?

I was a chronic worrier. I worried about everything. And if there was nothing to worry about, I would always find something. *Worry* was my middle name.

Several years ago, I suddenly realized that my worries had transitioned into caring concerns.

> Whereas worry begets misery,
> Concern begets joy.
> Whereas worry begets fear,
> Concern begets strength.
> Whereas worry begets anxiety,
> Concern begets peacefulness.
> Whereas worry begets restlessness,
> Concern begets calmness.
> Whereas worry begets depression,
> Concern begets hope.
> Whereas worry begets problems,
> Concern begets solutions.
> Whereas worry begets control,
> Concern begets faith.

I no longer waste my time worrying about petty things—things that are not threatening or disruptive, things that are not hurtful, things that pop up and get in the way of my carefully planned agenda. I no longer worry about what people think or say about me.

I am concerned about situations, feelings, needy people, hurting people, social concerns, those who think on a petty level, about my church and where we are going, and about those who do not know God.

I must have had an epiphany which released me from the curse of worrying.

It dawned on me that I have a partner in all that I do. Wow. God and I worry together, but not for long. Just long enough for Him to teach me and to assure me that He is always present; to hear my concerns; to advise me; to comfort me; to give me strength, wisdom, and courage; and to love me unconditionally through all things.

Rx: for Impulsive Behavior

The Silent Sunday Afternoon

It was Sunday afternoon and I did *not* want to go to another boring old baseball game.

I was surprised when my mom came outside where I was playing and announced, "I am going to stay at home today, Ellenor, so you won't have to go to the ballgame."

As soon as the words left her mouth, I had this sudden, strong desire to go.

Without thinking, I sneaked quickly into the back of Daddy's car, scrunched into a tiny ball, and covered up with the Sunday comics. Daddy climbed inside, drove a couple of blocks, and picked up Mr. Rob, his friend.

I was as still as the quietest mouse ... and suddenly very, very scared. "Oh my, what have I done? What am I going to do when we get to the ballpark? What will Daddy do to me? What on earth made me do such a dumb thing?"

Just as Daddy and Mr. Rob were getting out of the car, I jumped up like a jack-in-the-box and blurted out, "Here I am, Daddy!"

Those were the only words I spoke the entire Sunday afternoon. Daddy and Mr. Rob were speechless and in shock; however, Daddy quickly found his voice and let me have it with both barrels.

"Young lady, do you realize what you have done? Do you realize how worried your mother must be, not knowing where you are? Do you realize that you will be punished when we get home?"

I only nodded.

Oh, I was so scared ... Whatever had caused me to do such a terrible thing?

I remained silent. I did not ask for a drink or candy. I did not complain. I did not ask, "How much longer?" I kept my mouth shut for three long hours.

As soon as we arrived home, I jumped out of the car, ran around the house as fast as my little legs would carry me, and hid under a big bush, knowing that a spanking was waiting.

I heard Mother call, "Ellenor, come here right now! We need to talk." By this time, the tears were flooding the yard.

I learned later that, in the meantime, my wise mom had convinced Daddy that my fear of the long-awaited spanking had been enough punishment. And she was so right! I never, ever had done such a thing before and I knew, in my heart, that I would never, ever again pull such a stunt. I had learned my lesson. And besides, I don't ever again want to be quiet for three long hours!

July 1939 (I was eight years old.)

SECTION 3
LAUGHTER: THE CATALYST THAT JUMP-STARTS OUR HEALING SYSTEM

"Nobody ever died of laughter."

Max Beerbohm

Rx: for Memory Loss

The Little Boy Who Forgot

The family gathered around the kitchen table for supper: Daddy, Mother, and their two sons, ages five and seven.

The youngest was asked to pray the blessing. It was customary for a member of this family to pray at each meal. And he began to pray ... and pray ... and pray. The food was getting cold, but he continued to pray ... and pray ... and pray. Mom and Dad peeped at each other, wondering what they should do.

Finally, the little boy looked up and said, "I've forgotten how to stop it."

It was all they could do to keep from erupting with laughter.

Out of the mouths of babes ... This must be what the Bible means when it says to "pray without ceasing." How pleased God would be if we forgot how to stop our prayers. "And a little child shall lead them."

(A true story shared by dear friends.)

Rx: for Mental Stress

Kids Say the Darnedest Things

This is definitely an "Art Linkletter" moment

In the small rural town of one hundred and fifty residents lived a lady known, and loved by all, as Miss Ellen.

Miss Ellen had been ailing and, as was customary, most of the ladies in the town came over to check on her.

Now there was one older woman, who dressed rather plainly with brogan shoes and loosely fitting dress and had hair pulled back in a haphazard bun, who had also dropped by. She was called Miss Nellie, and Miss Nellie had a rather unusual and outstanding feature, especially for a woman, but one which the locals no longer seemed to notice. Miss Nellie had ... a very dark and prominent mustache, and for some unknown reason, she did not try to hide or eliminate it.

On this particular afternoon, Miss Ellen's five-year-old grandson and his mother had arrived for the weekend. Miss Ellen gave Clif a big hug and then proudly introduced him to Miss Nellie.

Well, Clif looked up at Miss Nellie with a very puzzled expression and then with childlike innocence blurted out, "Are you a man or a woman?"

His mom paled and didn't know whether to grab Clif and run or try to offer some incredibly forgiving remark to try to erase the awful faux pas.

Just when it seemed the darkest, all of a sudden Miss Nellie threw her head back and gave the biggest, longest, and loudest laugh you have ever heard.

Soon we were all laughing with her. She was not the least bit offended and had diffused this horrifying moment simply by laughing.

What a gift!

Thank you, God, for laughter!

1962

Rx: for Indigestion

My Dinner Guests
(Last Thursday)

I live alone, but I do not like to eat alone, so ...

As usual, I sat down in my big chair in the den, with supper on a tray resting on my lap, and I flicked on the TV. I reached for a juicy piece of chicken and placed it in my mouth just as the announcer came on with a message about—of all things—nasty toenail fungus. Just what you've been waiting to hear about while eating, right? He even went so far as to say, "Call today to uncover the truth about nail fungus, and you can get a free video. You can go barefoot without embarrassment."

Not too appealing, but it was soon over and I reached for a forkful of crowder peas. And then I saw this shot of people sitting in a room and talking when all of a sudden the guy on the sofa, with a painful look, lifted the left side of his somewhat plump posterior and a voice from nowhere gave a graphic talk about Preparation H.

Well, the crowder peas lost their flavor, but priding myself on my coping ability, I knew I had to persevere, and so I continued with my meal. (Though I must admit it was with a half-hearted effort, at best.)

Some apple sauce, a bite of bread, and back to the chicken. But wouldn't you know my suppertime was not to be spared? I found myself gazing directly into the face of a girl who was gazing directly into my face, and she had the nerve to begin reflecting on how your period starts really heavy and then gets lighter.

At that point, my taste buds (which have to get psyched up anyway to eat my cooking) collapsed in a catatonic state;

my hunger pangs were at once forgotten; my appetite was so traumatized that at this stage I wasn't sure if it could ever be resurrected ... even by a Hassell Church Homecoming spread.

Is there an answer to this demoralizing dinner dilemma? I suppose I could eat alone, but I would probably be resentful and tense, which would only cause other problems, such as indigestion and gas—not desirable—especially at mealtime.

I suppose I could mute each commercial, but I'm not the mute type, and besides, muting during mealtime would most likely manifest itself in a greasy mute button, and who wants that problem?

So, what do I do? I still sit in front of my TV, supper tray on my lap, like a wimp, intimidated by voices in a box—tense, gaseous, and with a greasy mute—but at least I'm not eating alone!

Rx: for Sins of Omission

Not All Cooks Are Created Equal

I flunked cooking—*big time.* It wasn't that I didn't try or that I didn't want to cook, but I truly *did not get it.* It was dangerous for me to be in the kitchen. Once, I accidentally set my kitchen on fire while heating oil to deep-fry some pecans for Christmas gifts.

The most blatant mistake occurred when I was proudly making orange balls for my son's party. (A two-year-old could have pulled this off—a real no-brainer.) When finished, I asked my son to sample one to see if they met with his approval. Just as I was passing the plate, I noticed (out of the corner of my eye) a box sitting right under my nose. I had left an entire box of confectioner's sugar out of my simple recipe. Believe it or not, the orange balls were palatable; my son gave a thumbs up and said, "Yes," and we did serve them. But first, we had a good laugh at my expense.

Can you find the moral of this story? My first thought would be that the cook should have read the recipe more carefully. However, another message jumps out at me: even though life does not always give us all the things we want, we need to make the best of what we have. We might be amazed!

Rx: for Aching Bodies

Ode to Old-Age Pain

At my age is it supposed to be this way,
A difficult ache and pain nearly every day?
"Oh, my aching back," you say with a groan
As you try to get up, accompanied by a moan.
My feet are all messed up with metatarsalgia,
And to dance with the pain is not so fun for "me-ah."
Arthritis is an issue and slows me down for sure,
But what can I do but grin and endure?
My blood pressure rises and sends me into a tizzy,
From struggling to walk while I am quite dizzy.
A pulled muscle in my arm is just another pain to bear,
From hauling a table up the basement stairs.
My neck is stiff; my eyes grow dimmer.
My hearing suffers—what a dilemma!
Reflux sets in and my stomach grows bigger.
Most likely that barbeque was the deadly trigger.
Beano is my friend and goes with me everywhere,
To save embarrassment and to purify the air.
And on and on it goes as I move through the years.
What do I do to allay these fears?
I just keep on going and pretend I'm a sweet young thing.
I figure that's better than being a whiny old ding-a-ling.

"And let me not lose heart and grow weary and faint in acting and doing right, for in due time and at the appointed season we shall reap, if we do not lose and relax our courage and faint."

Galatians 6:9

"No matter how old you get, if you can keep the desire to be creative, you're keeping the man-child alive."

Anonymous

Rx: for Aging

P.A.P.

What is this new disease called P.A.P.
Which comes uninvited to you and to me?
And no matter which doctor I go to see,
He always says I have this P.A.P.

It sounds so ominous that I tremble with fear
When this diagnosis is made, that I dread to hear.
"So what are the symptoms?" I timidly ask.
"To name them all," he says, "would be a mammoth task,
But if you truly want to know and persist,
I will give you my modified list."

The eyes grow dimmer and cataracts might appear.
Friends begin to whisper, and the TV you no longer hear.
Women will have hot flashes as menopause takes its stand.
And you think they're permanently attached to their always
waving fan.
Men begin to notice that the hairline is receding,
So they part it much lower with hopes of being deceiving.
But what is negative to the man makes the lady no longer a slave.
Much time is freed up because she doesn't have to shave.
Mysteriously, the hair that once covered her from head to toe
Has quietly disappeared and she didn't even know.

That the teeth begin to yellow and are in need of repair
Finds you spending more time in your favorite dentist's chair.
You suddenly predict the weather as your joints suffer and ache.
You remember when getting out of the chair was just a piece of cake.
Once, you were tall and then you began to shrink,
Until you can barely peek over the kitchen sink.

Incontinence sets in and the race begins,
Unless you put away your pride and grab a Depends.

With each step you take, your feet respond in pain,
And the friend you've come to treasure is your special walking cane.
Did I mention dropping things that fall from your grasp
When your fingers no longer maintain their usual clasp?

Sleepless night appear and you wrestle with the sheets,
And you get up in the morn feeling quite beat.
Eyelids start drooping and paunches jiggle.
Jowls begin sagging and upper arms wiggle.
"I've fallen, and I can't get up," you say as a joke.
Until you're the one who falls and you know it is "broke."

Did I forget to mention that we no longer remember names?
To introduce a friend is becoming an eternal pain.
But our exercises increase as we cruise from room to room,
Trying to resurrect where we left that infernal broom.

The list goes on and on, but I am sure you will come to see
That this part of the aging process is what I now call P.A.P.
But let us not forget, as dreaded as it may be,
That this alternative has been gifted to thee and to me.
So next time you greet your friends politely before you flee
Simply skip the formalities and say, "And how is your P.A.P?"

Suddenly, one day after I had become older, I began to realize that each time I visited the doctor and would ask, "What is my problem?" he would always say, "Oh, it's just part of the aging process." Since that was somewhat demoralizing and depressing, I decide to qualify my ailment with a more respectful and medically definitive name. Thus "P.A.P." was birthed.

Instead of whining about age-related problems, learn to laugh about them with your friends. They are in the same boat!

Think about all the good mold that laughter will bring!

Rx: for Double Vision

The Magnifying Mirror

I had a wonderful time in Columbia for the celebration of my friend's seventieth birthday. I stayed in a lovely hotel, but it had one drawback which I was forced to put on paper in poetry form.

Here we are at the Whitney Hotel.
Everything seemed to be going quite well,
Until I walked into the well-appointed bathroom
And my life quickly converted to gloom.
Over to the right, hanging on the wall,
Was a magnifying mirror, of all the gall.
Looking into it was my biggest error.
An old lady looking out filled me with terror.
I jumped back, not knowing what to do.
Would you believe ... she jumped back too?
So I looked more closely at this pitiful creature.
Ruts in her face formed her outstanding feature.
But somehow she looked familiar, as if we had met.
It must be a face you could never forget.
All of a sudden, on came the light.
With the revelation that gave me a fright.
For looking at this person, I could see
That this old lady was actually me.

God doesn't look at my "ruts." He looks at my heart.

"The Lord does not look at the things man looks at. Man looks at outward appearance, but the Lord looks at the heart."

1 Samuel 16:7

A Day to Remember

A day to remember—
How could I forget
How carefully I dressed
The occasion to befit?
My special black suit
Was worn with great pride
As I entered the church
And sat down beside
A lady dependable, sturdy, and well bred.
A good place to enjoy the program ahead.
At least, so I thought, and relaxed in my chair
As memories of yesteryear filled the air.
And next came the highlight of the hour.
A love feast was served for all to devour.
A more moving occasion you never saw
With the exception of just one small flaw.
Remember the lady I sat down beside.
Well, alas and alack, I almost died
When all of a sudden this well-bred chick
Lifted her cup with one heck of a flick.
And out of the cup and through the air
The cider was deposited most everywhere.
A splash on the program, the dress, and the hose
And some on the chair, the floor, and the toes.
We hastily wiped and dabbed at the mess.
My composure was weakening under the stress.
And all of a sudden from out of nowhere,
My black suit was covered by white cat's hair.
From whence had it come,
I looked up and down
To locate this thing, which my suit it had found.

Lo and behold, out of the corner of my eye,
A white furry thing I did spy.
I swiftly reacted and grabbed up my purse
To protect myself from this terrible curse.
As I raised my arm high in the air,
A meek voice emerged from the very next chair.
"Put down your purse and please take note.
This is no monster; that's my rabbit fur coat."
A day to remember, thanks to my special helper,
A lady none other than Joretta Klepfer.

This is 100 percent true and we still laugh about it after at least twenty-five years.

When the Roof Caves In
All Is Not Lost

In 2007, I heard a fascinating story that had occurred in 1987, twenty years earlier. Imagine my surprise when I learned the roof of my Ford Country Squire station wagon caved in one night when my youngest son Wes had borrowed it to attend a high school event.

What a relief to discover that teenage shenanigans were the reason rather than the dreaded auto accident parents always fear.

Now I know why I half-jokingly tell my three sons that I appreciate that they withheld some of their early years' experiences.

For some unknown reason, seven teenage boys decided to stand on the roof of my beloved vehicle. Almost immediately, to the shock and dismay of those seven teenagers, the roof of the car buckled and caved in. No injuries occurred, but the scene that evolved was both traumatic and high drama. Fear, anxiety, horror, and "What do we do now?" were first and foremost on the minds of all once the shock subsided and reality began to emerge.

Did I mention that these were all exceptionally bright young men?

They were well aware that to return home with the car in its current condition would definitely result in harsh disciplinary action from all the parents. This meant they had to come up with a workable plan at once or else ...

Putting their heads together, the seven boys devised what they deemed a brilliant idea. It had to work, and it required the effort and cooperation of each guy present.

Seven young men climbed into the wagon, laid down on their backs (much like a puzzle formation) in order to fit, lifted their legs into the air, and placed their feet at strategic places on the pitiful concave ceiling.

Simultaneous precision, time, and action were the miracle solution to this otherwise overwhelming problem.

My son began to count (so the story goes)—"One, two, three, go!"—and all fourteen feet gave one heck of a push to that maligned ceiling.

The results of brainstorming, fear, and teamwork paid off. Out popped, literally, the roof, leaving it with no hint of what had transpired.

The success of that mission was affirmed by the whoops of laughter that could be heard echoing throughout the city.

Don't we, as adults, experience our own roofs caving in sometimes? We may be overburdened with guilt, too many responsibilities, too much in debt, and a plethora of other reasons. And aren't we often guilty of trying to go it alone rather than reaching out for fourteen feet to help?

Never try to second-guess what your children might do, but do give them credit for the ingenuity they display when it comes to solving problems. Never underestimate their coping skills when under pressure and how they "usually" find an appropriate answer.

Assure them that we trust them to be the best person they can be and usually that trust will not be betrayed.

At this time in my life, all I can say is, "Thank God for strong legs and fourteen feet ... and the laughter that puts it all into perspective."

"We cannot determine the events of our life, but we can determine our response to them."

Anonymous

In My Eagerness to Please...

My oldest son, Clif, emailed me five days after my step-grandson's birthday, tactfully suggesting that I might like to send a check, since he was coming home for the weekend to celebrate.

Oh dear, I had forgotten that important occasion. On Saturday, at one p.m., I hurriedly wrote the desired check, found a card (but not a birthday card), wrote a grandmotherly note, sealed it, and dashed to the post office, having already missed the deadline for the next-day delivery.

I raced to the window and said breathlessly, "I must get this card to Spartanburg, SC by tomorrow."

"Well, tomorrow is Sunday," the postmistress proclaimed loudly enough for a deaf person to hear, "and there is no overnight delivery." Then, all of a sudden, as I was almost through the door, she yelled, "Wait, I believe I have found a way."

Needless to say, I was thrilled and relieved. At this point, you need to know that I love my step-grandson dearly and never would have him think otherwise.

The end result was that I paid $27.90 just to get a little lightweight card delivered on Sunday.

I raced home, emailed my son these words: "Do not, under any circumstances, allow Clay to leave tomorrow before three o'clock. The card will be delivered!"

My son emailed me back as if I were a child (I could almost picture the expression on his face.) "Now, Mom, you know there is no delivery on Sunday."

I politely emailed back (thinking to myself, "Won't he be surprised that his mom was able to pull off this feat.") "You are wrong. For $27.90 it will be delivered."

Oh, what a relief and what a joy I was feeling, knowing that my problem was resolved.

The next morning I dressed for church, followed by my usual ritual of writing the check for my weekly offering. I opened my checkbook and lo and behold, I went into shock. Staring up at me was the birthday check still in the checkbook!

I had no choice but to call my son and confess my terrible sin of omission. His calm reply was, "Mom, I don't know what the rush was, since I told you in my first email that he planned to stay for a few days." How had I failed to register that important information?

I went on to church and, of course, I had to tell my friends what I had done. I thought they would never stop laughing. Every time we met someone, they would look at me and say, "Ellenor, tell so-and-so about your grandson's check."

I suppose it was worth telling my secret faux pas because my tale of woe always evoked fits of laughter.

At that point, the only consolation was that I was helping my friends activate those much talked-about endorphins.

I'm still laughing at myself and thinking, "It's probably not going to be the last thing I forget." And it wasn't!

Rx: for Constipation

My Life: An Enigma of Scraps of Paper

The phone rings, and I answer it. The caller has important information for me which I write on the back of a used envelope. I tear it off and leave it on the counter while I tend to more pressing issues. A few hours later, I return to retrieve it, only to find it has disappeared.

A friend sends an e-mail which needs to be recorded on my calendar. Jotting it down hastily on a piece of paper at hand, I place it on a stack of other notes next to my computer for safekeeping. Two hours later, it's gone!

One of my boys calls to give me their vacation address. Frantically, I look around for some paper, any paper, to write on and discover a napkin waiting to be tossed. With frustration, I struggle to write it legibly, in spite of the letters spreading on the soft paper. The next day, I cannot find it.

A thought that comes in the middle of the night is scribbled, with sleepy eyes, on an old bill lying on my bedside table, where it is left until morning. Daylight reveals a brilliant thought is missing!

At least three times, I have visited the little shop down in the woods near the back of my lot to measure the cushion on a settee, only to have lost the paper I wrote on. My feet grow weary from the trek to and fro.

It's time to buy groceries—a page torn out of a small notebook receives the list of things I need to buy. It is tucked into my purse, or so I thought. Even Art Linkletter could not find this list.

Long hours are spent each day going through piles of paper, looking under chair cushions, revisiting pant pockets that I had last worn, emptying out trash bags, and yes, even hanging head first into dirty garbage cans just hoping to get my hands on that elusive piece of paper.

When did this evolution take place? When did I become this little old lady who is totally dependent on such a mundane, insignificant, unattractive, inexpensive thing as a piece of paper?

Do others see me as a senile older woman who lives in a world of notes on scrap paper? Have I taken on the persona of a vague, floating, out-of-touch personality who remembers only what is written down on a piece of paper that is lost? Am I referred to as "the lady who is always searching"? I wonder if I am sentenced to this lifestyle forever.

And then a horrifying thought crosses my mind. *What if I should run out of scraps of paper?*

I can only laugh.

SECTION 4
GOD'S AMAZING CREATION GIFTS

Rx: for Recognizing the Holy Ordinary

The Gift:
One of My Favorite
Christmas Memories

I love flowers, especially wild flowers, and prior to Christmas 1984, I was in the process of redesigning and adding to my wildflower garden.

While walking in the woods beside my home one day, I spotted the perfect stump, which I immediately pictured in an idyllic spot in my garden. I did casually mention this discovery to my husband during supper that evening.

On Christmas morning, while checking my stocking, I found a note suggesting that I look out the back den window. To my amazement, the huge, magnificently sculpted stump was sitting in plain view, now sporting a giant red bow. I was thrilled and couldn't wait to get outside to put my new treasure in its place of distinction.

What a wonderful gift and what a wonderful reminder, in retrospect, when all had quieted down, that we are surrounded by God's gifts and that they are all free, just waiting to be discovered, used, and loved.

Who would ever guess that an old stump could bring such joy and beauty to my life? And it didn't cost a cent!

"A gift is not a gift until it is given away with love."

An "Ellenor-ism"

Rx: for Unmerited Blessings

The Creature Gift

The quietness that pervades my house in the early morn begs me to tread softly lest I disturb the space within.

My silence, however, was quickly shattered this day by the steady, locust-like chirping that lured me to peek out the large bow window.

Rewarding my curiosity were several tiny, brown, speckled birds splashing in the pools of water collected in the giant hosta leaves. Apparently already bored, one hopped over to perch on the brick planter, only to be startled by another of God's creatures. A little sassy and confident chipmunk scampered up close to greet his newfound friend.

I watched, mesmerized, as they played hide-and-seek like happy children, in and out of the long, dense bed of periwinkle.

Peering out into the dimly lit day with eyes barely open, I was gifted with this incredible reminder of the magnificence of our Lord's creation—perfect in its smallest creatures as well as its highest mountains. A gift, unparalleled, yet often ignored and overlooked, replaced by the shabby, the flashy, the insignificant, the big and demanding, the unimportant, and the showy.

Two tiny creatures, God's gift to me today. No special occasion, for no special reason, and at no charge. And I have done *nothing* to deserve it!

"Today is the day the Lord hath made; let us rejoice and be glad in it."

Psalm 118:24

A Humbling Winter Storm

Looking out my window
in a white world,
cold, icy, threatening.

Sleet, peppering steadily
at my bow window,
tapping an ominous tune.

Trees covered in ice
heavy with their own fear
of bending and falling
onto the frozen earth below.

Wires stretching from pole to pole,
glistening and glimmering
from freezing layers of rain.

I, wrapped in my cozy cocoon,
savor the warmth of my happy fire
dancing to its own tune.

The wait and suspense grow long,
dreading that anticipated flicker
warning of what's to come.

Ah, sweet light that bathes my every move
that I've grown to expect as part of living,
yet its control slips from my grasp.

One quickly falling limb
and the snapping of a wire
change our lives in one split second.

From control to helplessness,
no power is mine
to flaunt before the world.
Infinity looms large,
and I am reduced to a humbling, small existence
from this lesson learned.

"Be merciful to me, Oh God, be merciful because I come to you for safety. In the showdown of your wings I find protection until the raging storms are over."

Psalm 57:1

The Second Storm

How bleak the world that I entered this morn.
Filling me with boding fears of the sharp, beating
sounds of a freezing rain
And brittle branches, bending and snapping
under the heavy load,
Playing a staccato-like song until the crescendo of
a huge limb or tree
    crashed to the earth below and ...
Blatantly breaks the steady rhythm and startles
me out of my gray, somber
    stupor
Strongly urging me to look for impending signs of
nature's unannounced attack
    on this place where I abide.
At least this time it only teased the walls as it
rushed to greet whatever was
    in its path,
Leaving the monotonous, staccato-like song once
again to fill my world
Until another resounding crash snuffed out the
lights and darkened all spaces,
Offering a black, barren void in which I was lost.
Briefly shaken by the sudden changes, I slowly
returned to the reality of
    my black world
And groped and stumbled my way down the dark
basement stairs to my mother's
    old oil lamp, hopefully with enough oil in its belly
To dispel the threatening shadows looming at me
from all sides.
The flickering match searches timidly for the

magical wick, straining to send its
feeble light into the room.
And I rejoice for even this tiny flame, which gives
back life to my domain.
Time almost stands still as I barely exist in this
"fireplace-warmed" room ...
Waiting, anticipating, hoping, praying for that
gloom-shattering burst of light and
the roar of voices from the forgotten TV.
A street light casts its usual glow on my front yard
outside the bow window.
Once again, I feel safe and secure and peaceful in
the noisy world I know best.

And yet, in the middle of this inflicted "near
darkness," there lives a silence so
beautiful, inviting me into its midst to simply
sit and listen and be.

"Though I sit in darkness, the Lord will be my light."

Micah 7:86

"There is nothing in all creation so like God as stillness."

Meister Eckhart

Rx: for Restoration

Sun and Rain

My eyelids, though heavy with sleep, are aware of the sun as my bedroom turns from blackness to a soft gray, fighting the light that tries to sneak through the closed blinds.

There is a strange, unidentified silence that greets me this morn. Something is missing from my early waking sounds and slowly, as I become more attuned to this new day, I identify the loss.

It's the constant pounding song of rain, often beating down on my flowers and bushes, bending them out of shape and then abruptly changing to a dainty pitter-patter or a slow, steady drone. Sadly, I no longer have a feeling of being wrapped in a cocoon of privacy.

I've come to expect this wet guest who has visited so long that it has now become part of my daily life, changing my plans with its unbridled determination. No weeding today, as they have grown tall enough to enter and win a blue ribbon at the state fair. No picnic as we scramble for shelter or look longingly in the refrigerator at the special fixings that must wait for another day. No going to the pool—the new bathing suit hoping to be shown off, the old body, however, gives thanks that it has escaped having its year-older ruts gawked at and commented on.

The house is bathed in a new scent of mildew and mold, and the clothes I reach for seem to be chilled and damp.

The umbrella even looks weary from its long hours of toiling and being dragged from place to place, hung on every strange hook, tossed under a dark table while I ate, and it never had time to dry.

How I've longed for the sun to once again enter my life!

And here it is, bright and cheery, bringing back the birds with their many songs, the flowers standing tall and the streets no longer glistening from the quiet splashing as they are awakened by the barrage of cars.

Yes, though my day is brighter and drier and my out-of-doors plans are no longer threatened, and my dry umbrella hangs quietly in its place, the rain has been a part of my daily breathing for so long that I wonder if I will remember how to exist without it.

Thank You, Lord, for sun and rain. Amen.

Written after several months of much rain.

Rx: for Vision Impairment

My Unexpected Blessing

My neglected flowerbed hung its head in shame
    at the emptiness it felt and for the weeds to be tamed.
Two white crepe myrtle bushes and a liriope border
    were the only things that bespoke of order.
Redemption was called for and I raced to the garden shop
    for that special flower to create the perfect backdrop.
Over to the side, a little white bush I did espy,
    the tag said simply, "I will attract a butterfly."
This most intriguing information definitely piqued my attention,
    for to add things beautiful was certainly my intention.
So home I did go with this little plant in tow,
    and placed it in the perfect spot where it could grow.
In no time at all, I was surprised to see,
    it had grown overnight and was pretty as could be.
Graceful white plumes filled nearly every branch,
    and huge yellow butterflies came and rewarded it with dance.

They flitted and pranced and tested each flower,
    and I thanked God for my unexpected blessing this hour.

He constantly nudges my busy and forgetful mind
    That the most wonderful gifts are the "holy ordinary" kind.

What joy I have had today watching the dance of the giant butterflies, and it didn't cost a dime!

Patient heavenly Father, I still don't always recognize a blessing even when You place it directly in front of me. Guess I'm too busy griping or too self-centered. Open my eyes as I plod through each day that I might see the good and the gift in the "holy ordinary." Amen.

Rx: for Purification

Reflections While
Sitting on the Pier

Water ... the smallest amount is like a magnetic
force, always drawing me closer.
It gifts me with tranquility and peace.
It reflects the surrounding beauty
    and my own image, if I dare to look within it.
It houses many of God's creatures.
It is life giving.
Water, the giver and sustainer of our physical
being,
The thirst quencher.
But then I am vividly reminded of the Living
Water,
    which only God can give, which Jesus offered
    the woman at the well.
How I thirst for this Living Water in my life as I
strive to deepen my relationship
    with God.
As I listened to the sounds of the overflow drain, I
was reminded of how water cleanses,
    how it washes away the impurities, how it
    makes us presentable before God.
Water is never still regardless of the season.
It is always alive!
It is always there, ready to fill me up.
Lord, You baptized me with Your water; You have
bathed me with Your water; You
    continue to offer Your water for me to drink.
I have been blessed today as I sit on the pier,
surrounded by this wonderful gift of water.

John 4:13–14 (Explanation for "Living Water")

Written while on a spiritual retreat at Camp Agape, North Carolina.

SECTION 5
LEARNING TO LIVE AND
LEAVE THE HURT BEHIND

Rx: for Depression

Hold My Hand

Come, hold my hand and walk with me as I climb the steep steps out of the darkness of imprisonment to freedom.

Escaping

    Releasing

        Awakening

            Forgiving

                Cleansing

                    Rejoicing

                        Thanksgiving

... from grief to coping

... from hurt to healing

... from sadness to joy

... from rejection to understanding

... from inhumanity to self-esteem

... from violence to peace

... from despair to celebration

... from darkness to light.

"But you, O Lord, are a shield for me, my glory, and the lifter of my head."

Psalm 3:3

Rx: for Emotional Pain

The Endless Tears

The falling of my tears from the grieving of my heart
Leaves me to wonder if they will every cease.
At rare times, only a few drops trickle down my dry, aging cheeks,
And I like to think the pain has eased,
    only to find the next time
    tears pouring forth like a powerful waterfall,
    leaving my eyes puffy and red.
And I wonder if there are any fluids left in my body
    in my grayish world.
I almost fear devastation from the flooding of my tears,
    washing over everything in their path;
    even the desert is no longer dry.
    And I cry out to be able to control this endless flow
That comes from the loss of my precious grandson
    and from the suffering of my children.
I know that as long as I hurt for them and feel their pain,
    the tears will come as a reminder of the fragility of life.
But my strength and hope come from knowing
    that in His time ...
God will wipe away each tear.

Loving and comforting Father, thank You for gently and slowly wiping away my tears, never chastising or rushing me. Thank You for teaching me as You comforted me that, in time, I would be able to cope and know peace once again.

"He who has a 'why' to live can bear with almost any 'how.'"

Victor Frank

Rx: for Breathing and Heart Problems

The Agony of Loss

Lord, how do I exist when I only want to grieve my loss?
How do I get out of bed each morning, only to face what I no
longer have?
How do I breathe when each breath struggles to call out to you,
my little one,
    knowing you're no longer here?
How do I face the simple chores that are part of my routine life?
How do I interact with my friends whose lives remain unchanged?
How do I stop the tears which unexpectedly interrupt with no
respect for time or place?
How do I exist when I only want to grieve my loss?

The hows and whys are too many and offer no words of comfort.
They only add to the agony that knows no peace.
How many times have I screamed at You, "Why me, Lord?"
And yet I know You are grieving with me as You wrap Your
arms around me
And Your tears flow and merge with mine, filling this space
where I live.
And I try to say, "Why not me, Lord?" but the words are still
bitter and refuse to pass my lips.
I know that somewhere, buried within the depths of my soul,
there is a tiny speck of light
    that keeps me from losing all hope,
    that keeps offering me a glimpse back into my world,
    that refuses to let me drown in my sorrow.
I know, Lord, that You keep reaching out to me through family,
a friend, yes, even a total stranger
    to show me Your love,
    to offer encouragement,
    to brighten that small speck of light.

I know You are not rushing me Lord. You're walking with me at my own grieving pace,

    ready to catch me should I become too unsteady.

I know You're slowly breathing life into my darkened spirit,

    without apologizing for this brief awakening,

    without feeling a betrayal to Jackson—the brightest of lights.

I know, Lord, that even though the pain often seems beyond endurance,

    You have promised never to give me more than I can bear, and that You will be with me

    every step of my walk.

I trust that because of Your incredible love and grace, my life will be restored and I will, once

    again, reach out to others who may need

    my compassion,

    my understanding,

    and Your love flowing through me.

Oh Lord, don't give up on me. I am truly Your servant. Just hold me in Your arms and gently

    nudge me back into the real world in Your time.

I love You, Lord. Amen, amen, and amen.

Out of this tragic loss, a mission fund was established for young people who could, otherwise, not afford to go on mission trips. The first year, $10,000 was donated.

The faith of Molly and Wes has become even stronger, and on Easter Sunday, three and a half years later, Molly told her story to the five hundred church members. She received a standing ovation.

I am sharing this so others might have hope in their darkest hour.

"I can do everything through Christ who strengthens me."

                                    Philippians 4:13

This was written after my five-month-old grandson had died from SIDS and I tried to express what I thought my children were experiencing, knowing I only scratched the surface.

Course 101: How to Wait
For a Loved One to Die

My head bobbles, rattling the newspaper
    I hold in my hand,
Startling me from my unplanned slumber that I *thought was impossible*,
    sitting in the hard hospital chair.
And I look over at the bed where my dear one lies,
    checking to see if the covers are rising up and down.
What else can I do?
I have never taken Course 101:
    "How to Wait for a Loved One to Die."
I watch as the nurses come in and out, taking vitals
    and now and then adding a new bag of that precious liquid
    that flows through the veins, giving sustenance.
I listen to the drone of the TV that my dear one likes to hear
    and wonder if he is truly hearing it,
    or is it merely comfort during these timeless days?
I wonder what he is thinking, if at all.
I wonder if he hears our words
    and strains to join in the conversation
I wonder what his hopes are in that withdrawn state.
Does he feel the selfish call of family and friends to hold on,
    to be strong,
Or does he long to succumb to the peaceful drifting
    that is gently tugging him to come home?
Perhaps our purpose is simply to be present,
    to hold a hand,
And, when the end is evident, maybe our gift should be the words,
    "I love you."
    "It's okay to let go."

Coupled with the prayers,
    "Lord, it's in Your hands."
    "Thank You for this special gift of life."
    "Whatever is will be."

Course 101: How to Wait for a Loved One to Die
The need is so great, but you do not yet exist
Even doctors and nurses have to wing it.
Granted, each person's journey is different—
    In length, in pain, in suffering, in cause, in treatment,
    and yes, in desire to live.
But there are similarities that speak to us
    sometimes in more subtle ways—
A look, a sigh, eyes refusing to open, a tear, agitation, stillness—
    many unspoken signs.
Surely, like everything else, these can be interpreted and shared
Clueing those waiting as to how to respond,
    what to say or do.

Course 101: How to Wait for a Loved One to Die
Where are you?
And why aren't you available?
With all the modern technologies and psychoanalyses floating
around,
There must be someone on a higher plane of intelligentsia
    who can prepare a syllabus
That will at least provide, if only in part,
    comfort to those who sit and wait.
Where are you, "Course 101: How to Wait for a Loved One to Die"?
    Where are you?

*Course 101 can be only God's words, God's presence, God's
promise, and our relationship with Him.*

Rx: for Hurting and Sadness

Solace for Sadness

Two crepe myrtle bushes, given by a friend
When pain was too deep to strain to comprehend.

Two crepe myrtle bushes, resting in their pots,
Waiting patiently to be placed in the perfect spot.

Two crepe myrtle bushes, their beauty still to be,
Yet their presence in my yard spoke words of comfort to me.

Two crepe myrtle bushes, now planted and waiting to grow,
As my pain still lingers. Will it never go?

Two crepe myrtle bushes, one late summer's day,
Beckoning me like a magnet to turn and look their way.

Two crepe myrtle bushes, now adorned in blossoms white
Have lifted my sorrow from darkness to light.

Two crepe myrtle bushes, given by a friend,
Bring comfort, hope, and love on which I now depend.

Two crepe myrtle bushes, just outside my door,
Bring solace out of sadness, forevermore.

Thanks again, my soul sister and college roommate, Gloria, for being sensitive to my hurting and lifting me up, giving me solace for my sadness.

Love you,

Ellenor

"We're healed from our suffering only by experiencing our grief to the full."

Marcel Proust

What's on the Other Side?

For several weeks, eight-year-old Jason had been acting very strangely.

He did not want to play baseball, his favorite thing to do.

He did not want to visit his best friend.

He did not want to go to a movie.

He did not talk very much.

He stayed in his room most of the time.

His mother became even more worried when she took a batch of his favorite chocolate chip cookies upstairs to his room and he politely said, "No, thanks."

What could possibly be wrong with Jason? she thought.

The next day, she took Jason to Dr. Shepherd, his pediatrician. (That's a grown-up word for a children's doctor.)

Dr. Shepherd checked Jason from top to bottom.

He looked into his mouth.

He looked into his ears.

He looked into his eyes.

He looked up his nose.

He listened to his heart.

He listened to his lungs.

He tapped his knees.

He did all the things a doctor usually does, and he did not find anything wrong with Jason.

So he told him that he could get dressed.

Dr. Shepherd knew that Jason's granddaddy had been sick and had passed away about the same time that Jason began acting differently.

"Jason," Dr. Shepherd spoke very gently, "before you leave, is there something bothering you that you might like to talk about?"

Jason, who had spoken only when spoken to, looked directly into Dr. Shepherd's eyes and blurted out, "Do you know what's on the other side?"

Dr. Shepherd, not sure he understood what Jason was talking about, asked, "What do you mean by 'the other side'?

Jason looked sad and said, "You know ... where they say my granddaddy has gone."

"Ohhhh," sighed Dr. Shepherd, now fully aware of what Jason meant but unsure of exactly how to respond. He first answered honestly, "No, Jason, I don't know what's on the other side."

"You mean you are a doctor and you go to church and you don't know what's on the other side?"

About that time, there was a loud thud against the examining room door, followed by a rather loud barking and scratching. As Dr. Shepherd opened the door, in charged Bailey, his giant, loving Labrador retriever, who leaped up on him and began licking his face.

After calming Bailey, Dr. Shepherd looked Jason straight in the eye and asked, "Did you see my dog?" "Yes, sir," answered Jason. "He didn't know what was on this side of the door. He only knew that his master was inside, yet when I opened the door, he ran in without being afraid."

"So, what's on the other side?"

"Jason, I don't know much about what is on the other side of death, but I know one thing for sure: that my Master, God, is there, and that's good enough for me."

Jason gave Dr. Shepherd a great big hug and walked out with a big smile on his face for the first time in weeks. He had his answer, and he knew that everything was going to be just fine.

This story was inspired by a simple e-mail message of unknown origin sent by a friend, which I have changed, added to, and made partly my own, with thanks to a stranger who had much wisdom and a powerful faith. In many of my workshops based on my book, Holding God's Hand: Teaching Children to Pray. *I have been asked, "How do I answer a child's question about death?" and I have found this story to be a wonderful response. Remember that young children want only a simple explanation.*

Rx: for Addiction

Frailties of the Soul

My soul is weak.
It turns away and shuts me out
as I strain to find that delicate balance
    between right and wrong
that was gifted to me
in my mother's womb.

My soul is at war.
Bitter conflict—its constant companion—
patiently waiting
its weakness to discover.

My soul knows no rest.
It struggles daily with the uninvited invader
who finds his way
through my locked door
And tempts me with its magnetic force
and promises of things beyond my reach
that draw me closer to the edge.
My footing is unsure and my decision
fills me with contempt.

Yes, my soul is weak
Yes, my soul is at war.
Yes, my soul knows no rest.
For my soul is not yet mine to be misused and abused.
My soul in all of its frailty needs only
To reach out and take His hand ... and surrender.
And then my frailties become His frailties and
My once empty soul is filled and fueled and freed.
My soul has become one with Him.

Patient God, how we must hurt You with our spiritual weaknesses. How easily we are persuaded to give in to the undesirable, to succumb to the easy way out. Strengthen our frail souls, and let us walk hand in hand with You. We love You, Lord. Amen.

Rx: for Strength

September 11, 2002

Dear Friends,

This morning, during my meditation, I felt the need to write my feelings of yesterday and to share them with those I care about. Hope you don't mind.

I must have shed a zillion tears. Somehow, a year later, the pain was greater. Reality was at the forefront. I hurt intensely to the very core of my being for every grieving person who had been touched by this horrific act of violence.

I hurt for the scars that are now permanently attached to our people and our nation and the other nations involved.

I hurt to think that fear is now a part of our lives, whether consciously or unconsciously.

And, to my surprise, it suddenly dawned on me that I probably hurt most of all for those who committed the acts of hatred. Hatred that is taught from birth. Hatred that has been passed from generation to generation. Hatred that can be easily directed by a few measly dollars and a false promise of martyrdom.

I hurt because these misguided children of God have never known reverence and sanctity of life.

I hurt because these people do not know the joy of living as caring, nurturing, loving individuals serving God and others without thought of self.

I hurt because I feel so helpless in changing these people of anger and destruction.

I hurt because I know God must be doubling over with pain inflicted by the atrocities of His own children.

And where does all this hurt and fear lead? How am I to deal with it? How do we all deal with it? What would Jesus do?

I believe He would first go off and pray, asking God for guidance. And then I believe He would go about his everyday life, teaching what is right by being a living example of love.

A simple solution to an overwhelming, complex, and seemingly irreversible problem, we think. A naïve, passive "Don't get involved" approach, it seems to be. But is it?

The most comfort and peace I have felt was at the prayer vigil service at First Lutheran last evening.

It came during the silences. Powerful silences ... moving silences ... connecting silences ... and silences filled with God's loving presence.

Though I could feel deep hurt, I was almost overwhelmed by the sense of strength and faith that seemed to pulsate throughout the large gathering of those who had come to mourn, to pay their respects, and be part of a faith community.

In silence, we processed out of the sanctuary, carrying lighted candles, led by a bagpiper who played "Amazing Grace." Our walk took us outside where we appropriately encircled the cross. With the service drawing to a close, we sang "God Bless America," we prayed, and we ended by passing the peace ... with lots of deep emotion.

What a blessing to live in a country of hope, of freedom, of peace, and yes, of love.

We have our faults and weaknesses, but they are forever overshadowed by the good we do and the strengths.

To this end, I pledge my allegiance ... one nation ... under God.

Amen.

The following poem, Transformation, was written after this letter and it I was asked to read it at the prayer vigil service at First Lutheran Church in Greensboro.

Rx: for Perseverance

Transformation

My spine is tense,
My jaws are clenched,
My hands are balled into fists,
And only this way I now exist.

I find it hard to feel
As I move in a daze.
My mind has ceased to focus
With man's changing ways.

This ludicrous, horrific act
Which made our world stand still,
Has left us numb to life
And paralyzed our will.

This evil force, which stalks us
And preys upon the world,
Has left its calling card,
Its fury to unfurl.

The losses still unknown,
Uncertainty rules the nation.
Emotions run the gamut,
Mourning this devastation

The flooding of the century,
From the shedding of our tears,
Washes o'er all our prayers
That briefly still our fears.

So what steps must we take
As family, church, and nation,
What steps to survive
This monstrous creation?

We know the answers
But we're slow to receive.
We've watched the answer
While seeing people grieve.

It's as clear as the soot
We see on their faces.
It speaks to us all,
The entire human race.
We've worked side by side
Digging through ashes and steel,
As night turns to day
And we no longer feel.

But we have to keep on going
And we must keep on trying.
We must put forth every effort
For the living and the dying.

For through this act,
We will never forget
Something has happened.
We must ne'er regret.

A nation has risen
And experienced rebirth.
A nation united under God,
The greatest on earth.

What we may not realize
Or are yet willing to face,
Through prayers and God's help.
We've become one color, one race.

This was written four days after 9/11 while my emotions were still raw, but my vision for our country was stronger.

Rx: for Holding On

My "Throw-Away" Day

I wander from room to room with conflicting emotions, harnessing my determined efforts to "throw away" that which is never used, that which clutters and has slowly invaded my entire domain, taking possession without even asking.

I wander from room to room, vacillating until I am dizzy from trying to decide where to begin, where to stop and "throw away" that first precious treasure, unused for years, which has claimed a spot in my closet and threatens me with unspoken words until I dare not "throw away."

I wander from room to room, bombarded with a potpourri of memories evoked from this reuniting with things long forgotten, things long unseen, but which are still attached to my soul with tentacles that render me helpless as they wrap around me when I try to "throw away."

I wander from room to room, finally stopping to make a pile of things I no longer need, only to discover that my pile is lost in its smallness and my reluctance to let go and "throw away."

What other things do we hold onto and are reluctant to let go that impact our lives?

<u>Keep</u>	<u>Throw Away</u>
Hurts	
Resentment	
Anger	

Try moving these and other things to the other side and feel your spirits lift!

Rx: for Fluid Retention

From Hostility to Hospitality

On June 1, 1998, I drove up my driveway, savoring the beauty of everything that I was seeing: the oak leaf hydrangeas, the giant hostas under the bow window, the now only green rhododendrons, the hemlock and dogwood trees, the towering maples, and more.

I pulled into the parking area, put up the sun shield, got out as usual, and was embraced with this joyous and overwhelming feeling of love for this space and place. It was not a worship kind of love for a "thing," and maybe love is the wrong word, but it suddenly dawned on me that I had entered a place that had experienced a rebirth. It no longer harbored ill feelings, fear, undesirable actions, hurtful words, distrust, and an un-Christ-like atmosphere.

Instead, there was this overpowering sense of serenity, cleanliness, purification, thanksgiving, and God's present that this was a refuge, if you will, a haven, a space just waiting for me, my family, my friends, and anyone else who might find his or her way here.

I knew I had moved from hostility to hospitality—a gift from God.

(Written two years after my husband and I separated.)

SECTION 6
FINDING YOUR OWN
TRUE SELF

Rx: for Restoring Trust

Who Am I?

Who am I?
Where am I going?
Who cares if I get there?
Who will know?

He will know.

I am His child.
I walk with Him.
He watches my journey.
He welcomes me there.

He offers His hand.
He gives His love.
There are no restraints.
He asks nothing of me.

How can I repay
This gift of His life,
Freely given,
No strings attached?

His overwhelming love
For my unworthiness,
His pain, His suffering
Beyond my understanding.

To make me free.

What can I say
In response to His gift?

Live as He lived.
My life for His.
Love as He loved.
Give as He gave.

Who am I?
Where am I going?
Who knows if I get there?

He will know ...
And care.

Lord, sometimes we feel so inadequate, so undeserving, and so unworthy, and we believe no one cares about us. How can we possibly feel this way when You have shown us a love that passes all understanding?

May we never forget that You know and love us in spite of who we are. Amen.

"Look at every path closely and deliberately. Then ask yourself and yourself alone one question ... Does the path have a heart? If it does, the path is good. If it doesn't it is of no use."

Don Juan, Yaqui sorcerer

Rx: for Restoring Faith

Reconnecting

How do I feel?
    I'm not sure.
Confused,
    Concerned,
    Anxious.
It's been so long.
    Too long.
I want to be friends.
    I want to be allowed to care.
    To do caring things
that friends do.
    To reconnect in the right way.
    To reach out.
To share.
To touch a feeling.
To touch a hand.
    To be able to find a new beginning.
    To encompass you in my friendship circle.
    To grow in that relationship
until trust between us becomes a precious gift
to be revered and nurtured.
    Can that be ...
    Can that bond ever be the same?
    No ... Can it be better?
    Yes, because if it comes to be, it will be blessed
    For its purity, its honesty,
its depth, its sincerity,
    And the desire to believe
that all things are possible
if we but believe and ask ...

Understanding God, it is so difficult to reconnect and trust once betrayed, but You have taught us to reach out in faith, to nurture the gift of relationship and to believe that all things are possible through You. May we be blessed with faithfulness. Amen.

Rx: for Dermabrasion or Derma-Peel

The "Unmasking"

After wearing a mask for a large portion of my thirty-two-year marriage, which ultimately ended in divorce, I was actually shocked at how many layers had accumulated and become almost impenetrable. The learning came in the "unmasking"! My true identity had been hidden for years in the form of unshared feelings, critical remarks, insecurity, the fear of not being a real entity, of being used and unloved, and a host of other damaging negatives.

As the layers started to peel away, real, honest feelings began to emerge, along with the realization that I was slowly becoming a whole, happy, peaceful human being once again.

Time, of course, had kindly diluted the painful memories, but other factors filtered in, slowly healing the perceived permanent scars. Several casual church friends embraced me and we became close friends; my spirituality group nourished my soul; my three sons and their families immersed me in more love than I probably deserved.

Many doors began to open, and with each opportunity and experience, another layer vanished as I relearned to focus on others and their needs. After training to become an adjunct chaplain last fall, I now serve part time at one of our hospitals, which has been like a homecoming for me. This was just one of several offerings that has blessed my life.

I learned to share my innermost feelings; I learned not only to reach out to others but to ask for help myself; I learned to praise, not to criticize; I learned to be more loving.

Most importantly, I learned that God had not forsaken me. It was I who had forsaken Him. In my tedious process of unmasking, I have learned that I was never hidden from God.

He was there, patiently waiting for me to reach out and ask for His help.

Lord, give us the courage to peel away the mask we have chosen to hide behind so that we might become the person You made us to be. Amen.

Rx: for Decision

Trust

As fragile as a butterfly's eyelashes ...
    one slight tremor and they quickly shatter
    into pieces so small
That they are lost in the dust
And then washed away forever
By the never-ending flow of tears.

It only takes one act of deception, one little falsehood, to wreck a marriage, to destroy a friendship, to cause the loss of a job, to discolor a reputation.

Is it worth it?

It can take a lifetime of tremendous effort to regain that trust.

Rx: for Multiple Personality Disorder

You Are an Original

"We will not compare ourselves with each other as if one of us were better and another worse. We have far more interesting things to do with our lives. Each one of us is an original."

Galatians 5:26, (The Message)

Have you ever wanted to look like someone else? Have you coveted the talents, personality, wealth, family lifestyle, spouse, or job of another person?

Have you ever wondered why God made you just the way you are?

Each of us is an original! An original is authentic, not a reproduction, a first form from which other forms are made or developed or imitated. You have heard the expression "They threw away the mold when they made Johnny."

Think about it. No one in the entire universe has the same set of fingerprints as you have.

Originals grow in value: an original painting, an original clothing design, an original of most anything, if kept in mint condition and not altered to be something it is not.

How often have you said, or heard someone say, "I was left out when God was passing out talents, or if I have a talent, I haven't discovered it yet"? Could we possibly, unknowingly, be confessing that we don't dare risk trying something new, that we lack the courage to explore new avenues, or that our fear of failing blocks opportunities? Or are we simply afraid of becoming involved? What a waste!

Conversely, know yourself. Don't pretend to be someone or something you are not. Don't be impressed with yourself.

Each of us must take responsibility for doing the creative best we can with our own lives.

Your phoniness or fake personality will trip you up and you will lose your credibility even with those you strive to be like.

God would not have made you the way you are if He had wanted you to be someone else.

How often have you heard these words uttered: "I wish my hair were thick like Betty's"; "Why can't I have Sue's long, slim legs?" or "If only my waist could be as slim as Mary's"?

We are our own constant, whining, ungrateful critics, picking and pecking away at ourselves until we don't recognize who we are or, more truthfully, who we were. In this new millennium, the buzzword is *cloning*, and that is exactly what many of us have been doing for decades: tirelessly striving to become a copy of another human being rather than developing what God has given us, which is the person we are and can be.

Accept who you are, who God made you to be.

Don't insult God by expressing dissatisfaction and demeaning His creation. Each time you criticize yourself, you are criticizing God's handiwork.

Rx: for Fear, Fatigue, Fulfillment

The Wreck

Jamaica, 1984 ... a head-on collision with a tour bus ... racing ambulances ... the emergency room ... and *fear*. Fear of the unknown, fear for my life and my husband's, fear of stranger faces in a different culture, fear of being alone. This aloneness was overwhelming, until on the third day two eighteen-year-old Jamaican women appeared at the door of my hospital room while clutching their Bibles. At first, I was frightened, having already been the victim of an attempted robbery in the emergency room. I quickly learned, however, that they could not afford to go to college but they had felt God's call to visit and minister to those hospitalized. They held my hand and prayed with me, the only foreigner in the ten-story hospital which had been stripped during a revolution. An unbelievable peace was mine, a gift from two young strangers, filled with God's love, who had surrendered to His will to serve.

For nineteen years, this scenario would creep into my thoughts, time and time again, but it wasn't until the spring of 2003 that I learned the reason why. I was totally unaware of the volunteer adjunct chaplaincy program at our local hospital until a church friend became involved.

Immediately, I knew without question that this was my calling. This was what I had been searching for. This was my homecoming.

Needless to say, training and graduation ensued and I began my journey as a volunteer, walking the halls, checking the nurses' stations to see if I was needed, going in and out of the many cubicles in the emergency department, connecting with those experiencing serious or life-threatening conditions, and always carrying a code-blue pager and the chaplain pager. I was there to respond to the needs of the patient, family, and staff. I was ready to talk, to hold a hand, to call a friend or family member, ready to pray, to just listen, or simply to be a quiet presence.

Fatigue follows these calls, but the joy of the homecoming and ministering to those in need far outweighs the physical, and I give thanks for being allowed this humbling gift of adjunct chaplaincy.

Two friends, my husband, and I were vacationing in Jamaica when the horrific wreck occurred. I still suffer from my injury, but being alive far outweighs the pain.

Rx: for Discernment

"Never Confuse Your Net Worth with Your Self-Worth"

I usually tune out TV commercials. 1. Because they are so loud. 2. Because many are offensive. 3. Because they are manipulative. 4. Because they often misrepresent the product.

However, when my attention was captured by the above statement, I immediately knew that this commercial was different and I could hardly wait until it came on again. It's surprising to learn that this commercial was advertising Jeep Cherokee, but it could have been any product.

"Never confuse your net worth with your self-worth."

How do you equate the value of self? What are the measuring tools that you use?

Material acquisitions?

Annual salary?

Clubs you belong to?

People you socialize with?

Size of your home?

Number of cars you own?

Trips you take?

Status in the community?

Are you happy with how it all adds up? Do you have peace of mind? Can you relax and enjoy what you have? Do you share your wealth with others? Do you associate with those who have less? Do you feel that something is missing in your life?

If so, where should you look? What plan of action would you have? Would it be as aggressive as your plan to succeed? Would you work, or do you work harder to earn more? Do you constantly look for more things to buy? Do you have trouble sleeping at night? Maybe you have headaches or tummy aches or simply feel anxious or stressed out.

Does any of this sound familiar? Have you ever thought about a different approach to living, to pursuing your dreams, and yes, even to changing your dreams and/or goals?

It will take discipline, it will take focus, it will involve taking a risk, it will take courage, and yes, it definitely requires help from a higher source, a higher being. So ... what do you think?

Are you man or woman enough to sign on to this new journey? A journey which will reward you with freedom, less stress, peace of mind, the satisfaction of putting others first, and, most of all, an overwhelming and humble recognition and acceptance of your own true self-worth, available only when you change.

With God's help, your greed becomes giving;

Your criticism, praise;

Your stress, peace of mind;

Your selfishness, sharing;

Your emptiness, love.

So what is your self-worth? You are an invaluable child of God, a humble servant who says, "Here I am, Lord, ready to serve. Use me."

Rx: for Flexibility

Subtle Changes

I travel through the day, now at a much slower pace,
And I wonder when I entered this reduced speed zone,
    so unaware.
Surely, there were early impending signals
    that forewarned, nuzzled, or demanded my attention.
Even my words and thoughts remind me of an old
phonograph
    winding down.
And my steps, instead of brisk and sure,
    sometimes shift into a shuffling mode.
Casually rising from a chair becomes an action of challenge,
    and I hope no one is watching this awkward transition.
"I'm sorry, but do you mind repeating that?"
    seems to be a staple in my current vocabulary.
I forget my best friend's name
    and am repaid with that dreaded icy stare.
My grandchild's birthday slips by undetected.
A gentle reminder later does little to salve my sorrow.
The subtlety of this change comes like a thief in the night
    with daybreak bringing the reality of missing treasures.
Finally, something clicks and honesty prevails over protest.
I swallow my pride and, with open arms, welcome with
thanksgiving
    this new stage of my life.

"For as he thinks in his heart, so is he."

Proverbs 23:7

*"All change incorporates loss, even those changes we deem to
be good and to our advantage."*

Anonymous

Rx: for Strength

Ode to a Lighthouse

You loom so tall and
    stand so proud,
And yet your loneliness
    washes over me.
You brave the winds and
    send back the waves.
You stand alone,
    a sentinel over your vast domain,
And yet I feel your hunger,
    your yearning.
You light the skies
    with your saving light,
Offering solace and safety to the lost and
    to those on the wrong path.
And yet you receive no comfort;
    no words of gratitude come your way.
You hold firm, never stirring
    and never shirking your duty.
And yet the loneliness prevails.
You dare to look down
    and risk seeing the world below:
frolicking children playing at your feet,
lovers whispering to one another in your shadow,
and the waves in their natural rhythm,
    flowing back and forth.
And yet in spite of your loneliness, you must smile ...
You have just received a gift,
a gift only you can see from your place in the sky.

Oh, lighthouse, you look so tall and stand so proud.

As much as we enjoy "outside praise" for what we have done, let us stand tall with pride and inwardly know the joy that comes from quietly being a force in someone's life.

My Anxiety Addiction
Anxiety at Its Best

Can anxiety become an addiction? Do we unconsciously come to depend on it to save us from certain situations in our lives?

Do we use it as an excuse when we don't feel capable, when we feel unknowledgeable, when we are not well prepared, when we are not sure if we can actually do what we've been asked and are expected to do, and when we feel uncomfortable in any given situation?

I am disturbed by the fact that I allow my anxiety to somehow take over and be in control of my feelings and my life. It is reprehensible to me that I let myself reach this uncomfortable mental state. Perhaps it's the "not being in control" that is most disturbing to me.

Usually, my breathing is shallow, my chest is tight, and an uneasy feeling that something is not right pervades my being.

I hate these times! Maybe my faith and trust is not as strong as I think it is or as it should be. Not in my control! What does that suggest? Is there some reason that I can't relinquish these feelings to God? Am I afraid to let go—completely—so that it's entirely out of my hands, that only God in His infinite wisdom and grace can offer this life to me, absent and apart from this malady anxiety?

But for that to happen, God tosses it back to me and says, "Okay, I am willing to do my part, but you must be willing to let go and trust me enough to accept this gift of life without anxiety, this life free from fear, tension, nerves, worry, apprehension, trembling, and sleeplessness. Can you do that?

Can you open your tight fists and give your anxiety to me with the understanding and knowledge that I love you? I do not want to see you suffer. Remember that with me, all things are possible."

Amen.

More thoughts about The Anxiety Addiction:

Does God offer me another way of dealing with this problem by making me look inward and examine my feeling more closely? Or am I not trusting of people to whom much has been given, specifically doctors who have been blessed with the gift of healing?

Why must we still place such a stigma on emotional and/or mental needs? Why must we hide these problems? Why are we afraid to ask for help? Perhaps we are embarrassed and fear others will think that we are weak, that we don't want to admit that we are not in control. Perhaps we think if we do nothing it will just go away. (Wishful thinking.)

So we often wait, instead of seeking treatment immediately as we would for a broken bone, a virus, or any other ailment— yes, even those of far less consequences.

What is that old saying? "Pride goeth before a fall." God wants us to put away our foolish pride and admit our weaknesses.

Remember what He says: "My grace is sufficient, it is enough. My strength comes into its own through your weakness."

We need to be accountable to ourselves, our family, and others, as well as to the Lord.

Lord, reveal to me how You would have me deal with this problem, and I will try, with Your help, to do as You say. I love You, Lord. Amen.

SECTION 7
RELATIONSHIPS

Rx: for Unclogging Arteries

Do You Truly Call Me Friend?

Do you truly call me friend
        when my thoughts
        fail to follow your thoughts
And my desires are not your desires
And I recognize and express
        my feelings as a different person?

Do you truly call me friend
        when I unknowingly offend you
        and speak words that are misunderstood?
Do you quickly drop the gates
        barring my entrance,
        or
Do you truly call me friend
        by ignoring the unlovable,
        forgiving the small stuff,
And quietly brushing away the obstacles
        Reaching out and accepting me, in spite of ...

Thank You, Lord, for the gift of true friends. Amen.

*"A true friend will see you through when others see that you
are through."*

                                        Robert Louis Stevenson (paraphrase)

Rx: for Weight Loss

I Forgive You

Three little words.
Three little words that we are reluctant to speak.
Three little words which can
    control a relationship,
    change a lifetime, and
    cause God to smile.

Do we secretly enjoy punishing someone for whatever he did to us, withholding our forgiveness? Are we afraid that if we forgive he will think we are a pushover and will repeat the same offense again?

The biggest obstacle that dictates our response is waiting for the offender to say, "I'm sorry" or "Will you forgive me?"

But aren't we taught that we can forgive people without them knowing? Yes, we can forgive them in our hearts rather than carry the burden around with us. It will weigh us down, gnawing at us until we have become depressed, until we have developed some physical problem, or until it turns us into an unpleasant personality.

Three little words ... an enormous gift.
Three little words ... which will give you freedom.
Three little words ... which will cause God to smile.

Help me be a blessing and example to others by saying, "I forgive you."

(The pounds will melt away!)

When Someone Deeply Listens to Me

When someone deeply listens to me,
I am filled with an overwhelming sense of awe
    ... and perhaps a wee bit of nagging doubt.
Dare I trust ... dare I let go
    ... and feel this gift so precious,
or should I tuck a bit of myself away,
lest there is betrayal lurking out of sight?

When someone deeply listens to me
    ... and I know it is real,
Words spoken become almost an unnecessary
nuisance.
Understanding replaces the struggling
    ... and the silence washes me in its beauty
Until I can barely keep from shouting.

But I dare not ... for my gift might vanish.

Listening is a precious gift!

Rx: for Relieving Stress

My Hairdresser's Haven

Sometimes a hairdresser/stylist is the most special person you can know. Petite and attractive, almost sixty (which you'd never believe), Diane always welcomes me with a smile as I crawl into her chair of distinction each Friday morning.

Diane is not only my hairdresser, she is my confidante, my mother-confessor, my advice-giver, my listener, my spiritual advisor, and I claim her as my friend.

I really don't know much about her life outside the salon except that which she opts to share with me. I know that she has a husband, children, stepchildren, and grandchildren to whom she is devoted. And I've met her cute little mother, who Diane diligently and lovingly looks after.

I have learned some things about Diane through our weekly conversations—that she is a gardener, from all reports a good cook, a loving wife and mother, and most importantly, a child of God. She is a warm, loving person who loves her church and takes an active role in its life.

Among other things, I feel free to discuss and share spiritual thoughts with her and am amazed at her insight.

On a more frivolous side, we both admire and enjoy unique jewelry, not to the extent of coveting but just from the standpoint of enjoying wearing and appreciating its beauty and design.

She teases me about not doing my hair at home, and I quickly and pitifully respond, "I just can't do it." Maybe that is my excuse because otherwise I would not find such peace and joy at the end of my always busy week each Friday without a visit to my hairdresser and friend, Diane.

It's a time for which to give thanks and to treasure. Diane, thanks for being a constant in my life and for always being you.

Love you,
Ellenor

Rx: for Behavior Modification

Bloody Battles in a War-Free Zone

"How stiff the air," said the child
    as he entered the room
And sensed the glaring sadness
    and ever impending gloom
That lived within these walls
    ... so intense and so strong
From the bloody battles fought there
    ... all the days long.

The husband and wife, alias father and mother, rarely speak without anger in their voices. They are notorious for putting down (ridiculing) each other and their children. The atmosphere within the four walls called home is gloomy, unpredictable, and often volatile.

Friends have begun to drift away. The children are afraid to invite their friends over lest Mom and Dad might erupt and embarrass them. They stay in their rooms more and more, trying to escape this thing that has happened to their family.

The light has gone out of their lives. "What has happened to our once happy family?" they whisper to each other. The joy, the laughter, the fun at mealtime, the anticipated outings, and all the other things they enjoyed as a happy family had vanished. Where had the love and caring gone?

More families than we can imagine are suffering from this malady, which I have chosen to call "reverse transformation." It might begin with just one unkind word or remark, without the privilege of retraction or apology. Added to daily, with other doses of unkindness, sarcasm, and ridicule, it grows from one debilitating word to an uncontrollable and abusive monster.

By this time, however, the parents have become conditioned to this practiced behavior and have no idea what damage and hurt they are inflicting on these precious children. If they are aware, it has become such a part of their everyday lives that they are prisoners of their own behavior and do not know or have forgotten how to reverse this situation.

Are we, too, guilty of this behavior? Perhaps not as full-blown as this mother and father, but the potential is present.

One slip of the tongue, then two, then three, then ...

Dear God, help us to be aware of the power of words, to think before we speak, and to let our words reflect only the love You have shown us. Let our children and others see the Christ in us.

We love You, Lord. Amen.

Rx: for Focusing

"Prayer Fastens the Soul to God"

Macrina Wiederkehr, in her book *A Tree Full of Angels,* quotes Julian of Norwich. "Prayer fastens the soul to God." What an extraordinary statement! What a thought-provoking statement! What a profound statement!

It has become the catalyst that gifted me with a better understanding and a longing to be more intentional in my prayer life with our Lord.

When we truly learn to pray, the distractions no longer demand our attention; words come more easily without straining for perfection; the sometime-dreaded silence wraps us in its profound presence. The masks and shields fall away, baring our nakedness and vulnerability without shame. An unknown force may draw our knees to the ground as newfound humility incapacitates the usual anticipated protest.

Our very being receives the "other" as easily as two clouds propelling toward a collision course only to quietly merge, magnificently becoming an entity of such magnitude that even "The Great One" smiles.

Prayer is the connecting force that gives direction and meaning to our lives, support for our actions, healing from suffering; peace from accepting, and joy from embracing.

Yes, Macrina/Julian, prayer truly fastens the soul to God!

"Do not worry about anything; instead pray about everything."

Philippians 4:6

Rx: for Reconnecting

A Friend Is Forever

I found this piece which I wrote when I was young and straining to be poetic. Though feeble in my literary attempt at the time, I do believe it conveys the true meaning of friendship and hope you will agree.

> A friend is forever and then and now.
> A friend is understanding the why and the how
> Of a trivial thought or a serious decision
> With sincere interest and no hint of derision.
> A friend is a helping hand in time of need
> No matter the length or weight of the deed.
> A friend is strength when you're feeling low,
> Pushing and assuring where'er you may go.
> A friend is faith when yours has failed,
> Praying and leading you back on the trail.
> A friend is laughter reaching out to give
> A moment of happiness, which you can relive.
> A friend is honesty when all others shirk
> And say false things to cover the hurt.
> A friend is listening with ears opened wide
> To uncover the feeling you've hidden inside.
> A friend is forgiving when some wrong you have done,
> While others may question or wonder or shun.
> All of these things are ours 'til the end.
> Thank God ... for having you as my friend.

Written to a life-long friend who had stopped connecting. After reaching out, I received her welcomed call.

Rx: for Procrastination

Time

Time ... as elusive as a delicate snowflake
    drifting from the heavens,
Defying me to capture it for one brief moment.

And, with face upturned,
    I stick out my tongue, evoking childhood memories.

Only now, the thief of reality upstages me
    in my futile straining.

Time ... gifted to me,
    with no money-back guarantees, no promises, no
instructions.

Time ... mine to savor, to shape, to spend, to waste, to enjoy
    in unquestioned freedom.

And I, in all my humanness, stumble down my selfish path,
suctioning it up with the speed of a jet in flight.

Time ... where are you?
    I feel you slipping through my gnarled, wrinkled hands,
and I wish that I had touched you
    with the gentleness of the snowflake.

*"Time has no divisions to mark its passing. There is never a
thunderstorm to announce the beginning of a new month or
year."*

Thomas Mann

SECTION 8
STORIES WHICH TOUCH MY SOUL

Rx: for Humility

I Came To Dance

In April 2006, I was in Las Vegas competing in a national dance competition when my soul was touched by one of the contestants.

A young lady who had been in a serious car accident was partially paralyzed and dependent on her wheelchair for mobility. She rolled onto the dance floor accompanied by four instructors. She could not stand alone. Kris used her arms as they maneuvered her chair to the music. But my world stood still when they lifted her up in the air and over their heads in a horizontal position. What freedom she must have felt. What joy!

The dance ended; Kris received a standing ovation. I almost ran to my room and, upon entering, my tears freely flowed. It was at that moment that I wrote the following poem, "I Came to Dance." I shall never forget Kris and what she taught me and the rest of the world that special day—about courage, faith, hope, and yes, humility.

> Lord,
> I came to dance ...
> > to spiral, to twinkle, to show off my steps.
>
> I came to dance ...
> > Only with thoughts of winning and wearing
> pretty dresses and seeing friends.
>
> I came to dance ...
> > But instead, you gave me Kris,
> who in a brief time has inspired me with her
> presence.

I came to dance ...
> But she has taught me courage and patience
> and hope.

She has touched my soul with the joy on her face
when she glides her "dance chair" across the floor
and lifts her arms gracefully to the heavens.

I came to dance ...
> And I received more than self-gratification

and medals and prizes.

I came to dance
> And I was humbled and reminded, Lord,

that I can truly dance ...
But only if I dance with You.

Rx: for Adaptability

A Precious Christmas Memory Christmas Plans Go Awry

My mother had been in a car accident, which left her in the hospital with a broken pelvis. The doctor, however, thought she would be able to come to our home for Christmas.

But on Christmas Eve morning, I received a call saying that she could not travel. What a shock at that late hour.

With only a few hours to get packed—clothes, gifts, food—pick up the turkey, and gas the car, I was breathless and fatigued by the time I got the kids dressed and we piled in the car, wondering what I had left behind. It looked as if everything we owned had joined us for the ride to Hassell.

After the store closed that evening, my husband and oldest son packed all of Santa's gifts, including the hamsters and their cages, into his car to transport to Mother's house.

On the way to Mother's, the children were obviously concerned that Santa would not find them and they continuously asked how he would know.

We arrived at a pitch-dark house with no one to greet us ... It was eerie and sad! There were no Christmas decorations, no lights, no tree, no manger, no gifts, no candles in the window, and no Mother with open arms.

As soon as we got inside and deposited our luggage, I raced upstairs and found an old tinsel Christmas tree in the closet, along with the crèche and Santa climbing a ladder.

The tree was placed in front of the double windows in the living room. The crèche went to the den.

Everyone was exhausted; the kids were sent to bed early, and we waited for Santa.

The next morning, two young children, a teenager, my husband, and I crept downstairs to see if, in fact, Santa had figured out our location.

The sign awaiting us was breathtaking and brings me to tears still, as I write. The entire tinsel tree was ablaze ... It glistened, it glowed, and it brightened the entire room, reflecting the sun coming through the windows. We were in awe! What a magnificent and glorious gift, and we did not need costly lights and ornaments and garlands. We only needed the gift of God's light. I was indeed humbled by this reminder and grateful to our changed plans.

As soon as the children had spent some time with their surprises, we drove the seven miles to the Robersonville Clinic to see Mother. The rules were relaxed that Christmas morning, and we were all allowed to go in and celebrate Christmas with her.

I have never forgotten that glorious tinsel Christmas tree blinding us with its brightness and its beauty.

It now lives in my attic, and one day I may bring it down and place it in front of my own window, knowing that God continues to gift my family with His glorious light!

My Unexpected Gift

It was September 1952. Excitement and fear were emotions that attacked and controlled my very being on that long-anticipated day many, many years ago.

My usual bouncy walk had slowed almost to a halt as I climbed the stairs leading into the small country schoolhouse.

It was my first day as a teacher—a young twenty-year-old music teacher fresh out of college, who dreamed of transforming the world from drabness to beauty, from sadness to joy, from hurt to healing, and from the ordinary to the extraordinary. I envisioned myself as a pioneer prepared to gift these children with the unfamiliar world of great music.

Having grown up in a little town only four miles away and with no formal music in the school systems, I was well aware of the crying need to introduce these boys and girls to this new world. I dreamed of leading them to a place where they could experience, if only briefly, a beauty they had never known. Beauty of a different nature. Beauty which could not be found in the drudgery of working in the tobacco fields or digging potatoes down on all fours. Beauty which could not be found helping Mama can vegetables in a hot, unair-conditioned kitchen where water usually had to be pumped or drawn from a well.

I was aware that most (at least 98 percent) of these children were familiar with only three musical instruments: the piano, the guitar, and the fiddle. Local church and country music was the music known to most. And just think: I was going to be the deliverer, the hero, the savior (if you please) of these children I perceived as deprived.

I finally made it to the classroom with sweaty palms and unsteady legs, trying to mask my sudden lack of confidence with a voice that I hoped reeked of bravado.

The children were well behaved, typical of the '50s, and seemed to enjoy whatever I offered.

Days quickly turned into weeks, and soon the Christmas season was approaching, which translated into programs that were created, directed, and produced by yours truly, the new music teacher.

By this time, however, I felt that I was making progress. Already I had prepared my students for the North Carolina Symphony concert, which was to be held in the nearby town of Robersonville.

They had learned to recognize all the instruments of the orchestra and were familiar with all the pieces to be performed.

Thinking that the bus ride would be the highlight of their trip, I was thrilled and amazed at their eagerness exhibited during the question-and-answer session of the program. All hands flew up, waving back and forth, ready to express their newly acquired knowledge. Needless to say, I was so proud of these boys and girls, and they were so proud of themselves.

My pioneer spirit continued to find its way into the classroom as I tried and used many unique and challenging methods to pique and keep the interest of my students.

We began to practice for our PTA Christmas program, and of course, we were expected to include the ever-popular "O Holy Night," which I had chosen for the fifth grade class to sing.

The first time they sang it all the way through, I nearly lost it. Coming from the back of the middle row, an unidentified voice captured high C with such purity and beauty of tone that Pavarotti, in all his fame and glory, would have bartered his soul for that sound.

My heart resonated with such joy and awareness of a gift so rare that I was left speechless and wanted to selfishly bottle that moment and never let it go.

Tears threatened to spill down my cheeks, and when I realized who the singer was, I was even more moved. It was the small, frail, young boy in the faded overalls, the one who was so painfully shy.

But that day, he did not sing softly as usual. That day, he sang as if he were alone on a stage for all the world to hear. This once-in-a-lifetime voice, this unknown, this small child unaware of his own gift ... And sadly, I (the only trained musician) was the only one there who understood and appreciated the depth of this gift we had been given.

Unfortunately, I taught there only a year, and now my seventy-five-year-old memory cannot bring forth the name of that dear and talented student.

I wonder if he lost that angelic voice as he entered puberty or if he still sings with the greatness and beauty so few have ever possessed.

In retrospect, evaluating my first year as a music teacher, I can honestly say that yes, I briefly transported these young boys and girls to another world where beautiful music reigned and instilled in some of them an appreciation.

But that is not what I remember most. No, I can still hear the glorious voice of that small fifth-grade boy who taught me humility. His unexpected gift was a blessing far greater than anything I could possibly offer. It was a powerful reminder that God does not discriminate when handing out His gifts, and that they may be found in the most unexpected places.

And for that year and the lessons learned, I will be grateful forever.

If anyone who was in the Hamilton Elementary School in 1952–1953 knows this young man, please contact me.

Rx: for Color Blindness

Loving Lina

It's hard not to love Lina when Lina loves everyone.

At age eighty-three, Lina's health offered her no choice but to give up her apartment and move into a health center.

She had worked in my home for forty-two years as a "household engineer" and often as a babysitter. My three sons claimed her as their playmate, their confidante, and their surrogate mother. I claim her as my friend. She is African-American, I am white, and we all are family.

My last name is Shepherd, and when touring the selected health center, I was shown several rooms from which to choose. A soft-spoken white lady in her eighties, named Hazel Shepard (spelled differently), occupied one of the rooms. Intuitively, I knew that Hazel's room was the right choice. Lina and Hazel bonded at once, but they still call each other Mrs. Moore and Mrs. Shepard. If you ask why the formality, they break into a fit of laughter like two teenage girls.

They enjoy everything together. They go to meals together, they watch TV together, they laugh together, they share gifts of food together, and they sit peacefully and in silence together.

I do not believe that either of them has ever noticed that they are of different colors.

Recently, Lina stayed in bed all day, barely speaking. Mrs. Shepard went to the nurse's station to express her concern and was told angrily to go back to her room.

She sat for three days in a hard chair facing Lina's bed, never leaving the room. Her meals were brought in. She refused to turn on the TV for fear it would disturb Lina.

Thankfully, the charge nurse on a different shift assessed Lina's condition and called to inform me that even though Lina was being treated for a UTI (urinary tract infection), it was her opinion that she should be admitted to a local hospital.

At the hospital, Lina was diagnosed with pneumonia, UTI, and a stroke, which had left her right side paralyzed and her speech impaired.

Hazel was devastated when she heard the news. She said repeatedly, "I miss her so much." Her son called to say that his mom was very upset.

While in the hospital, though unable to speak, the nurses would comment, "Lina is so sweet." Her loving nature reaches out to touch anyone in her presence.

Loving Lina is so easy, and as for Lina loving others, it's what she does effortlessly and unconditionally.

And my thoughts keep returning to *what if?* What would this world be like if all people, though different, could share and love each other like Lina and Hazel, or as they say, Mrs. Moore and Mrs. Shephard.

"And the greatest of these is love."

"Ninee," as she was called in my family, died on December 15, 2009.

My Garden Bench Bargain

On Tuesday, January 21, I ventured out to the local shopping center while searching for that special after-Christmas bargain.

Upon entering one of my favorite shops, my eyes rested immediately on a copper-like garden bench. It was barely visible, almost hidden by a group of pictures displayed on its seat.

I moved on to check out the sale items but felt compelled to interrupt a young salesman to casually inquire about the price of the bench. There was something magnetic about this bench that kept drawing me back to reexamine it. The appeal grew stronger, and I became convinced that it belonged in my garden.

The fact that it was in a large, flat, rectangular box and had to be assembled did not discourage me or curb my desire for that unneeded purchase.

After rushing home, I tore into the box, pulled out the parts, and quickly put them together. You would have thought that I had constructed the Eiffel Tower. I was like a proud mother longing to show off her first arrival.

Adrenalin kicked in and I lifted the bench as if it were weightless, carried it across the yard, and deposited it in a recently cleaned-out, informal bed watched over by St. Francis of Assisi. There, a shepherd's hook holds four different bird feeders nestled under the redbud tree and overlooks a clump of blooming helebores (Christmas rose.)

I sat down very quietly on my new treasure as if my very presence in the garden would disrupt the entire scheme of nature. The sun was warm and comforting, and I drifted into a brief relaxed state. My reverie was short lived as I was interrupted by an unexpected gift, and I sat barely breathing or blinking.

It was if a production had been planned for my benefit alone. The opening was ever so dramatic. Crows from high above announced the cast with their attention-getting caws. One by one, the different actors and actresses came on stage until they formed one spectacular cast. I saw the handsome red-headed woodpecker flitting back and forth from tree to feeders; eight gentle, velvety gray mourning doves strolling proudly across the lawn to center stage; small finches, no longer their brilliant yellow, putting in an appearance, along with the chickadees, the wrens, and others with lesser roles. They darted through the green foliage, some too quickly to identify.

Several came so close I could almost reach out and touch them. For once, the squirrels and rabbits stood on the sidelines, seemingly as fascinated by this interaction as I was.

Suddenly, it dawned on me that while I sat on my new garden bench, grinning like a Cheshire cat, tears were streaming down my cheeks—tears of profound joy for having been gifted with this private showing of God's creatures coexisting and interacting peacefully. They shared the same space, ate at the same table, and joined together in a mixed chorus that brought me to my knees. I have never known a more profound peace simultaneously with the awareness of God's overwhelming presence.

My guilt feelings for the unneeded purchase were quickly forgiven and replaced with intense feelings of gratitude. How would I ever have experienced such a primal yet perfectly orchestrated performance that captivated my attention and catapulted me into an arena above and beyond any other?

My newly purchased copper-like garden bench was indeed an unexpected bargain!

Rx: for Welcoming Strangers

The Man on the Bench

Let me tell you a story, a true story.

Several years ago, a homeless man appeared on a bench in a park located near a shopping center. A stream ran through a culvert behind the bench and an overpass loomed in front of the bench. Here he lived. This was home. This was where he ate his meals. This was where he slept (under the culvert, I was told). This was where he read the newspaper; this was where he existed. Hot, cold, rainy, windy—this was home.

One day, I realized that he no longer resided on the bench. And then I read that he had gone to the hometown of his sister in another state but was treated badly by unkind individuals and forced to move on.

In May, for some unknown reason, I began to think about this homeless man, and each time I drove by, I would glance over to the bench, almost feeling his presence. One day I even slowed down, hoping that he had returned.

On the evening of May 20, I picked up my pen and pad and began writing, "The Man on the Bench." I am still puzzled as to why.

On May 21, a friend who was living through a traumatic and horrific separation asked me to meet her at a restaurant in the shopping center. I suggested another place, but she was insistent on her choice.

We ordered our food and sat for over an hour talking. It was an intense and emotional conversation for my friend in which I was deeply involved. Suddenly, I felt as if someone else was with us. I felt a presence. I looked up, and there was "the man on the bench" choosing the table directly across from me, almost within touching distance. With the sunlight coming through the windows, there was almost an aura around him. Without thinking, I blurted out, "Oh, my God!" Alarmed, my friend said, "What on earth is wrong?" I reached into my purse and pulled out my pad, which I held up for her to read the words: "The Man on the Bench." When I explained who he was and that I had just written the poem the night before, she too was overwhelmed.

I could hardly breathe or speak. After recovering somewhat, I got up to leave and stopped beside his table, gently touching his shoulder. I said, "I'm so glad that you are back. I have missed you. I want to tell you about a strange thing that happened. Last night I wrote a poem about you and I called it, 'The Man on the Bench.' I am glad you are back home."

He smiled and softly said, "Yes."

I smiled and walked away.

Ode to the Man on the Bench

The man on the bench ...
Just sitting.
Leathered by the elements,
Sitting quietly,
Layered in clothing, well-worn.
Sometimes reading,
straining with weakened eyes
to see the fine print.
His umbrella opens,
The only roof to keep him dry.
A daily walk
With bagged possessions in hand,
To the shopping center nearby,
Where food is offered
And a gas station restroom awaits.

The man on the bench ...
Befriended by a church,
Now sits each Sunday within its walls,
On a back pew,
And on raw, bitter days,
A hotel room they freely give.

The man on the bench ...
Once a college graduate, a revered professor,
Respected for his brilliance,
Now homeless,
A bridge to sleep under, a bench to sit on.
His possessions, reduced to a bulging knapsack,
Slowing his pace, heavy with the weight.
His face, almost blank of expression,
Now and then softened,
As you glimpse an intended smile.

The man on the bench ...

No longer there in his home,
And I, with all my jumbled, conflicting feelings
Mourn this loss,
Humbled by his gentle, accepting soul.
My life transforms briefly to the simple
And I wonder what I have missed
As I keep watch
For ...
The man on the bench.

A Life I Never Knew, but One That I Loved

I quietly entered the small, sterile hospital room,
Its space filled with life-giving contraptions,
And I saw the lifeless body
    almost consumed by the tentacles reaching out
    from their respective origins.
No eyes opened to acknowledge my presence.
No voice responded to my greeting.
No nothing—just silence—
Except for the eerie sounds of the machines.
Am I welcomed here in this almost surreal space?
Dare I, a stranger, impose on this patient's
    time of transition?
And yet a force stronger than I
    compels me to stay.
I feel the need to touch, to connect, to interact
    with this once vibrant being.
I am drawn to the bedside.
My hand reaches out to touch the brow, and
    my other hand gently strokes the arm.
And almost unknowingly, I begin to speak, to pray
    with unplanned words, words that just come,
Words which I pray will bring comfort,
    words which will give strength,
    words which will give hope—
    hope for a better life—
    words that say, "I care,"
    words that say, "God loves you."
I rise to leave this room with no words of good-bye,
    or thank-you-for-coming, or a smile—no nothing.

And for the next several days,
    I faithfully check the obituary page
To see if the light has gone out,
If the machines have been turned off,
If another person has left this world,
And I give thanks for a life I never really knew ...
    but one that I loved.

Written after I visited a hospitalized man who was close to the end of his life and had no family. I felt a connection and a need to stay awhile.

My Name Is Shepherd

My name is Shepherd, but do I live up to it? Is it a burden or a gift?

I often wonder if people, especially Christians, have certain expectations of me when they hear my name, or does it float right over their heads?

Do they consider my name as belonging to one of a lowly profession, one in which I must deal with the out-of-doors, the elements: cold, sleet, snow, storms, and often ravishing heat? It is a profession in which I deal with dirty, filthy, straying animals who sometimes mindlessly wander away, often causing me to have to roam and search in places where I would otherwise never step foot: steep cliffs, briar patches, rocky terrain, and places so isolated that I fear that my life could be threatened.

Do they make fun of the clothes I must wear and which, by the end of the day, are usually covered with dirt, sometimes blood, and the stench of cleaning out and walking through the excrement of so many? My fingernails are jagged and stuffed with dirt. Perhaps my very being is offensive to them.

Am I beneath their social status? My salary is one of the lowest; my lifestyle is scorned by those who spend their time climbing the proverbial "social ladder."

Little, if any, formal education is required for me to excel in my profession, so I don't qualify in the eyes of the norm as scholarly.

Do they see me only as a lowly creature doing a job with all of its degrading aspects that somebody had to do and then dismiss me from their world of straining and striving for social, cultural, and financial success?

Oh, how I wish they could see and know the *real* me, the joyful me, the contented me, the peaceful me, the grateful me, the blessed me. They would most likely scoff if I described myself in that way.

If only they could be outside with me to see God's glorious world in all its splendor and power, especially when He paints it onto so many magnificent canvases. Canvases covered with snow, glistening with the many icicles hanging from any place they can find to cling, shafts of lightning that flash through the sky, the earth alive with the fresh smell and shiny vegetation and clean streets that come only after the sky opens up and dumps its waters, the heat which sometimes seems unbearable but warms us and causes our plants to grow so that we might fill our stomachs and enjoy the beauty. Perhaps together we could take care of God's creation.

Oh, how I long for them to see how comfortable I am in my unattractive clothing—loose, sturdy, protective and certainly not fashionable. I wish they could know, as I do, the joy of having a grateful, loving lamb come up and rub his dirty, and often unpleasant, wet body against mine, begging for me to love him and giving love in return—no inhibitions, no barriers, no holding back, and really, no hidden agendas—just the sharing openly of a mutual love.

Oh, how I wish they could come down from their intellectual pomposity and crouch to the level of communicating with God's lowly creatures, where they would only need to know how to make soft, caring sounds and use gentle, simple words of assurance, encouragement, and welcoming to draw my sheep closely to them.

Oh, how I wish their monetary yearnings would be replaced with the joy that comes from doing something that you enjoy; that gives you great pleasure in serving, in doing for others; that brings you great contentment and peace for doing your best, for taking care of others and knowing that you are quietly walking in God's footsteps.

Oh, how I wish they could feel and know how blessed I am to be able to reach out, to care for, to serve, to love, and to be loved in return.

What more could I possibly want?

If lowly means loving, so be it!
If dressed shabbily means giving, so be it!
If lacking knowledge means caring, so be it!
If searching for the lost means joy in the homecoming, so be it!

Lord, You have given me so much more than I deserve. Let my name, whatever it is, forever be a reminder of who I am, who I should be, and with Your help, who I can be: a good shepherd.

Amen.

Ralph Waldo Emerson wrote, "God evidently does not intend us all to be rich, or powerful or great, but God does intend us all to be friends."

SECTION 9
ARE YOU READY?

ARE YOU READY?

Are you ready to grow your own penicillin?

Have you learned to look for and focus on the good mold?

Try keeping a "good mold" gratitude journal each day. You may be amazed how God has blessed you in so many ways.

Now, "dose" others with your good mold. Share your blessings.

Only by giving yourself away can you have a healthy and happy spirit!

CPSIA information can be obtained at www.ICGtesting.com
Printed in the USA
LVOW132336250113

317310LV00001B/46/P